CW00386267

EGON
Ronay

Egon Ronay

This edition first published in 2011 by Newbaz Ltd

Designed by Lizzy Laczynska

A CIP catalogue record for this book may be found in the British Library.

ISBN 978 0 9570460 0 9

Printed and bound in England by
TJ International Ltd, Padstow

EGON
Ronay

EDITED BY PETER BAZALGETTE

Preface

On grainy film you see a sprightly teenager walking confidently across a field in summer sunlight towards the camera. He is wearing a smart white shirt and as he approaches he straightens his bow tie and smooths back his hair. The year is 1929. The youth, so concerned about his appearance, is the 14-year-old Egon Ronay. The cameraman is his father, a wealthy Budapest restaurateur. This cache of home-movie images from the Ronay family archive also shows his opulently dressed relatives enjoying holidays in Monte Carlo. As the sole heir of the family business Egon Ronay could look forward to an assured future. But that is not how things turned out.

Obituary columns are compelling to read at the moment. Many of those whose lives are chronicled represent no less than the history of the twentieth century. Egon Ronay is a case in point. Born in 1915, he trod a path through some of the most significant, dramatic and traumatic episodes of that eventful epoch.

Egon arrived during the First World War as a subject of the Austro-Hungarian Empire. It disintegrated three years later and then he grew up in an independent Hungary. This was one of a number of Central European states that existed only briefly between the two world wars. To us today they seem to have a distant, magical quality, captured, perhaps most brilliantly, in Patrick Leigh Fermor's books (a man with whom Egon corresponded). For Hungary this was shattered once and for all by the Germans in 1944, quickly followed by the Russians and then 30 years of enforced hibernation behind the Iron Curtain. With the Ronay family's considerable hotel and restaurant business in ruins and the state in the process of being subverted by the Soviets, Egon left for Britain in 1946. He was 31 and already married with a family.

There then followed an extraordinary seven decades of advising, enticing, imploring and browbeating the Anglo-Saxons to pull up their culinary socks. From managing London restaurants in the austere London of the 1940's, to launching his own eaterie and then a food column in a national newspaper in the 1950's, through the Egon Ronay Guides' heyday in the 1960's and their controversial public food campaigns of the 1970's, to the founding of various gastronomic academies and the championing of British chefs in the 1980's and consultancies for airports, pubs and motorway service stations in the 1990's and 2000's, to finally the establishment of his own website. And had we got the message by then? Not to Egon's satisfaction – he continued to be a relentless exposer of the careless, the mediocre and the plain cynical right up to the end.

This was Egon Ronay, spanning 95 years, from the twilight of one of Europe's last great empires to the consumer-led, online, citizen-asindividual era of the twenty-first century. This book contains essays about Egon from those who knew him at all the stages of his technicolour life. József Zimányi was at Catholic school with him in the 1920's. József died, aged 95, shortly after he had made his contribution to this book. Paul Fabry, now 93, and Egon were young men about town enjoying the charmed life of 1930's Budapest together. Antonio Bolza was an inspector for the Ronay Guides in the 1960's, as was Michael Edwards later. Francois Brocard, Godfrey Smith, Nick Ross and Dante Campailla were Egon's dining companions, the last doubling as his lawyer as well. Richard Pennycook hired Egon to tackle the catastrophe of British motorway service food. Notables as far apart as Michael Winner, the film director, and Lord Bramall, the Field Marshal, were admirers. All pay tribute here to a remarkable man with an extraordinary spirit.

I would like to thank the members of the Ronay family who have assisted in the preparation of this book. Egon's second wife, Barbara, made his business archive and various photographs available to me. Edina Ronay, Egon's fashion designer daughter, also generously offered photographs and other fragments from the family albums. And Esther Ronay, his other daughter, a film maker, translated József Zimányi's piece and provided many insights. This book is dedicated to the Ronay family.

Peter Bazalgette | SEPTEMBER 2011

Editor's note: for the tricky matter of accented names, we have used them for Hungarians but not for naturalised Britons or Americans, and we have kept them when quoting the original text of menus.

Contents

Field Marshal Lord Bramall, known as Dwin, was Chief of the Defence Staff at the time of the Falklands War. He has since served as Lieutenant of Greater London and President of the MCC. He was a member of the British Academy of Gastronomes.

József 'Joci' Zimányi was born in Budapest in 1916 and went to school with Egon Ronay. He studied law and later served in the Hungarian army, including on the Eastern Front. From 1950 to 1976 he was head of the legal department at the state-owned Csepel Iron and Metal Works. Joci introduced Egon to his first wife. He died in September, 2011.

Paul Fabry was born in Budapest in 1919. He served in the Hungarian army and as 'Captain Gombos' helped resist the Nazis. He became a politician after the war but, as an anti-communist, emigrated to the US in 1949. He later founded The World Trade Centers Association.

Antonio Bolza became a Ronay inspector at the tender age of 21 in 1965. He later ran his own successful publishing company in Munich. In 1994 he bought the magnificent Castello di Reschio estate in Umbria which he continues to restore with his architect son.

A HUNGARIAN BRIT OR A BRITISH HUNGARIAN?
Peter Bazalgette

Peter Bazalgette worked as a television producer, being responsible for several food programmes. He's also the author of three food books and writes a *Financial Times* column. He presented a BBC Radio 4 documentary about Egon Ronay and was Chairman of the British Academy of Gastronomes.

A LIONHEART WITH A STEEL-TRAP MIND
Michael Edwards

Michael Edwards is a wine and food writer specialising in Champagne and Burgundy. His authoritative guides to Champagne have sold widely and won awards. He was a Ronay inspector and later a member of the British Academy of Gastronomes.

THE LAWYER'S LAWYER
Dante Campailla

Dante Campailla was the senior partner of the leading London solicitors, Davenport Lyons, and remains a consultant to them. Dante acted as Egon Ronay's legal adviser and was also a member of the British Academy of Gastronomes.

INKFISH RISOTTO AND FIN DE SIÈCLE BRANDY
Nick Ross

Nick Ross is one of Britain's most respected journalists and broadcasters. He worked for most of the BBC's current affairs flagships as well as presenting *Crimewatch* for 23 years. Nick was a member of the British Academy of Gastronomes.

EATING WITH EGON
Francois Brocard

Francois Brocard was an investment banker for Morgan Stanley and BNP Paribas. He is a member of Club de Cent and has contributed to the Oxford Symposium on Food and Cookery as well as the 2006 *Oxford Companion to Food*. He was the Egon Ronay Guides Customer of the Year in 1994.

AN INSPECTOR CALLS
Richard Pennycook

Richard Pennycook is Finance Director of the supermarket group Morrison's. He has worked at companies as diverse as the RAC, Bulmers and Laura Ashley. As Chief Executive of Welcome Break he hired Egon Ronay to help improve its food and service. He was in the British Academy of Gastronomes.

LE STILTON ANGLAIS
Godfrey Smith

Godfrey Smith is a distinguished author and journalist. He edited the innovative *Sunday Times Colour Magazine* in its early years, giving the likes of Jilly Cooper their first commissions. He was married to a food writer and belonged to the British Academy of Gastronomes.

THE MAN WHO TAUGHT BRITAIN HOW TO EAT
Michael Winner

Michael Winner is one of Britain's most prolific film directors, with the three *Death Wish* movies being his best known. He is also the trenchant and occasionally dyspeptic restaurant writer for *The Sunday Times* and has campaigned tirelessly to win recognition for the bravery of the police.

The very first Egon Ronay Guide, published in 1959 and covering restaurants in the London region only. It was an instant hit.

Above: Egon Ronay as a toddler around 1918 with the first of many uniforms he would be obliged to wear.

Right: Egon, right, and unidentified tennis partner on a trip to Britain in the 1930's.

Above: The Belvárosi, the Ronays' flagship restaurant in Budapest before the Second World War.

RIGHT: Party revellers in pre-war Budapest. Egon is middle row & second from right, his first wife Edith is front row & third from right.

ABOVE: Egon and Edith's clandestine wedding in Budapest. Egon's father is far right; Edith's father didn't know it was happening.

RIGHT: Egon's parents. After the war they were stripped of their restaurant and hotel business and left Budapest penniless.

ABOVE: In the Hungarian army in the late 1930's. Egon, second from right, is wearing a sergeant's uniform.

ABOVE: The Ronay apartment, early 1945. A group of leading citizens celebrate the departure of the Germans after the brutal siege. Joska, Egon's trusted waiter, is serving (*collection-Fabry*).

RIGHT: Starting a new life in Britain with Edith and daughters, Esther and Edina.

LEFT: Jean Gardes, Egon's prized French chef at The Marquee in Knightsbridge , 1953-6.

BELOW: Cary Grant and his third wife, Betsy Drake, dine with Egon and Edith in the 1950's.

ABOVE: Egon and his team of inspectors in 1969. Chief inspector Major Gray is far left.

RIGHT: Egon and Barbara, his second wife, designing one of the guides.

LEFT: Egon and Barbara returning from Capri, a favourite holiday destination.

BELOW: Egon never lost his acute palate, even in old age.

RIGHT: The subject of the first portrait Barbara ever painted. Egon had been dining at L'Ambroisie in Paris (© *Jessica Strang*).

Introduction

FIELD MARSHAL THE LORD BRAMALL, KG, GCB, OBE, MC

What is it that would first come to mind when reflecting on Egon, such a dear friend to so many? Well, I suppose it would have to be his great courtesy and immaculate food manners.

Yet our main memories of him must revolve round our admiration and respect for his formidable knowledge about everything to do with food – its production, preparation, cooking, serving and consuming and his unrivalled experience over the whole field.

This he had acquired initially as a trainee in his family's chain of restaurants (six in all) in pre-war Budapest, including its prestigious city centre flagship seating over seven hundred, which after further training around Europe he was to go back to and run. Then, after 1946, when he got away from Communist-dominated Hungary to come to this country, he built on and passed on that experience to an ever-widening following. He managed, over 16 years, three central London restaurants and opened one of his own. He wrote copiously for the press on food and tourism as a critic and assessor, and also as an author of many books on these subjects. He came into particular prominence with his original restaurant guide which, bearing his name, he published for over 30 years and was so widely admired for its fairness and perspicacity. He also became the natural President of the British Academy of Gastronomes, to match the prestigious French one.

Indeed, through the rest of his long life he was courted on many sides for his judgement and advice on how catering standards could be improved. It did not matter whether it was in the field of expensive restaurants, aspiring to qualify for a coveted Michelin star, or friendly, less expensive neighbourhood ones, or even in the areas of the one-time despised airport or motorway catering. All these, at one time, benefited from his leadership, encouragement and thoroughly practical advice, to the great advantage of the British public as a whole.

As a result, his personal contribution to the raising of standards in British catering, once at a very low ebb but now generally recognised as around the 'top of the tree', was formidable. It was therefore a travesty that, despite receiving many international awards, he was never accorded a national honour appropriate to his standing and his important work in his adopted country.

Egon always expressed himself, whether verbally or on paper, cogently and coherently and always with dignity. He was never, despite his unrivalled knowledge, overbearingly arrogant. He was strongly opinionated but not self-opinionated. He always showed an understanding that others might have different views, in which he always expressed an interest. This is what made him such a delightful companion, conversationalist and raconteur.

He wore his advancing years so well that he appeared almost indestructible, but now that he is gone, well into his nineties, it is certain that those of us who knew him will never forget him. His achievements with the food industry and culinary art will, thankfully, be long lasting – something he himself might have found difficult to acknowledge, given his campaigns for ever-higher standards and his lifelong struggle against complacency.

My Oldest and Dearest Friend

József Zimányi

E gon Ronay and I were in the second year at Budapest elementary school when we met. By chance we sat at the same desk. We were in the same class in senior school too and finished our studies at university at the same time. We became very close friends. Egon was a very hard-working and extremely active young man and during our years at university he also obtained a diploma from the business college. Young people at the time lived a completely different life and their interest in culture was also entirely different. We had only heard of television and even radio was not as popular then as it is now.

Entertainment for young people consisted mainly of ballroom dancing school leading to countless balls and other parties. Girls could only socialise if chaperoned by their mothers. But when they walked home from the dancing school, the mothers and daughters were sometimes joined by a few of the more forward boys. This is how

Egon met Edith Rudolf and he became her constant companion. Even in their early twenties, if they intended to marry they would need their parents' permission.

Edith's father, Papa Rudolf, was expressly against this and it was out of the question for him that the Rudolf and Ronay families should be associated in any way, for he was proud of the Christianity of his forefathers. Although Egon was brought up as a Catholic it was known he had Jewish antecedents. The lack of parental permission held up any marriage plans. However, Papa Ronay had excellent connections and personal relationships as the owner of the Belvárosi Cafe. There was a Hungarian law that allowed the registrar to sign a marriage certificate without parental consent in exceptional circumstances.

This is how they married without parental permission. It is quite another story that within a few weeks the objecting Papa Rudolf became one of the most regular customers at the Belvárosi Cafe. All was forgiven, it seems. The young couple lived in a beautiful flat and it was obviously a successful marriage. Soon two girls were born, one after the other.

After his matriculation exams, Egon had to do one year's compulsory military service. He ended up in the same mounted artillery regiment as Paul Fabry. The latter hardly needs any introduction and has, of course, also contributed to this book. Egon and Paul became good friends and later, due to his rank in the army, he managed to help Egon to avoid prolonged military service during the Second World War. Fabry also helped Egon to leave the country with legally issued passports and settle in England with his whole family in 1946. By the time we were in senior school, Egon had been to London several times and would come back saying that compared with Hungary, life for the middle classes in England was much more agreeable.

In our youth in Budapest we used to wander around the city together. Once the two of us arrived at the funfair, where one of the entertainers stood in the goal as if he were a goalkeeper. When someone scored a penalty the 'goalkeeper' received 20 fillérs (pence); if he saved it he got 40 fillérs. We got talking to this man and he told us that he was living in utter poverty.

He was the same age as us, but he was still attending the last year of elementary school. He was in fact providing for his whole family. His father was an alcoholic, his mother a washerwoman and there were five children.

Egon felt very sorry for him and wanted to give him 10 forints (pounds). But the young man turned down the money, because his employer forbade him to accept any tips. He didn't want the public to think that this entertainment was put on by beggars. Egon later gave him a job as an apprentice waiter. That's what he was like. Very generous and helpful if anyone needed his support.

Egon and his family lived in Budapest till 1946. During this time, Egon was constantly looking for some special activity. He edited a student newspaper, directed student films and organised a ping-pong competition in every school year. One of the participants was our classmate Peter Bauer. Despite his short stature and heart problems, he almost always won the championship. This was the Peter Bauer who moved to England about the same time as Egon and his family. The big difference between them was that until the day he died, Egon spoke and wrote perfect Hungarian. Peter Bauer, on the other hand, seemed to want to forget his Hungarian origin and was, of course, eventually appointed to the House of Lords.

We often went to the skating rink in Budapest where Egon, Edith and I skated nearly every day. On one such occasion, a young man unknown to us made an offensive remark about the lady in our company. According to Hungarian custom at the time, such an affair must end in a duel. The duel was a strange institution. It was strictly illegal, but elite society considered the offended party morally dead if he did not demand justice. This was such a strict moral code that, for example, professional soldiers and even reserve officers were demoted if it was discovered that they had declined when challenged to a duel. The formalities were carried out by chosen seconds, who decided whether pistols or swords were required. They also had to establish whether the offence was really so serious that it required a duel.

In our case, since there were two of us, we drew lots and I was picked to fight for our 'honour' (Egon's account of the incident is in Nick Ross's chapter). Egon was to be my second. It is ridiculous but it was natural in those days. On the day of the duel we agreed that Egon would come and fetch me by car at 6 am so that we could be there punctually at the agreed time. Being any more than five minutes late meant that the person concerned didn't want to take part in the duel. Such faintheartedness would be held against him. Unfortunately I overslept on the given morning and we were almost late. This was the only time during my friendship with Egon that we had a serious quarrel. In retrospect he was right to upbraid me. I should report that the the duel took place with a satisfactory outcome for all parties and no one was hurt.

At the end of the Second World War, after the occupation by the

Russians, Egon was forced to join up as it had been announced that the families of deserters would be held responsible. This was in 1945, when as a high-ranking political official Paul Fabry was able to form an independent squadron with the help of false documents. He led it as an actual lieutenant (with false papers, of course). Its members consisted exclusively of deserters and similar men. Fabry named the squadron Special Auxiliary Squad and Egon became a member for a time. Rather ostentatiously he was taken from his flat every morning in 'handcuffs' by a fellow soldier to this fantasy squadron. It is worth noting that this company saved the lives of a great many people and this is how Fabry helped Egon under Russian rule. Looking back it is a funny thing that this charade needed to happen at a time when so-called democracy existed in Hungary for two years. In fact, under the Soviets, it was only the combination of Fabry's inventiveness and Egon's shrewdness that kept us all alive and out of jail.

I was not surprised that, giving up everything at home, he moved to London in the spring of 1946. I was doing my military service, so that I only met Egon once or twice when he came home on visits as a British citizen. Despite this, our friendship was extremely close and we maintained it mostly through correspondence.

Egon was an extremely precise man in every way. When he arrived in England, not only did he succeed in getting a job with the help of friends, but in a relatively short space of time he became one of the leading lights of the catering industry in London.

After the Ronay family left, we corresponded frequently. This did not diminish our friendship. On the contrary, it had the effect of reinforcing it. I could recall many stories and events we shared, but time is limited and would not be enough for even a tenth of them. Hungary lost an extraordinary person with Egon's death, but sadly he was less well known here than he deserved.

⬥

There follows a poem sent to Egon Ronay by József Zimányi in 2005. It started out in the form of poetry but reads, in translation, more as prose.

We were children together, we went to school together,
We were young students together and studied at the universities,
We moved in the same social circle of boys and girls,
You remember the little blonde you pursued vigorously.

And the city was vibrant and pleasant to live in,
The residents were happy and the Pest citizen witty,
Post-war life was full of hope and merriment,
A cafe on every corner, music coming from the windows.

We went skating in the winter, played tennis in the summer,
From time to time a good ping-pong player would emerge,
How many games of robbers we played, Kari, Lothár, you and I,
And what a splendid view from the roof of the Ritz Hotel.

The Gerbeaud in the City Park is but a memory now,
In its place a soup kitchen awaits its penniless guests.
I will never forget when Makay was sick all over you,
And you ran along Váci Street to change into clean clothes.

Makay waited at least two hours I remember,
Because it is no bad thing to apologise,
And when you returned very angry,
He had the gall to be patronising:
"This wouldn't have happened if you had sat behind me,
Make an effort and you will lag behind me yet."

In senior school you started a newspaper,
And asked me to be your editor,
The paper was called 'Hungarian Student'.
It ceased, as sadly it did not have much success.

Then our group planned to make a film,
So we shouldn't be left behind on the cultural scene,
The title of the film was 'The Lindbergh Baby Kidnap',
And I write of our adventures here below.

The Hommonais' villa was to be the location,
And we would all have excellent roles,
But there was no obvious candidate to play the baby,
The group thought it would be a little dangerous.

To save himself, the kidnapper, hotly pursued,
Throws the screaming baby from the car.
Laci Homi finally suggested his little sister.
The two-year-old was happy to accept the role.

When their mother found out what we were planning,
A certain private part of ours was suddenly in great danger,
Then she told us what she thought of us,
Unfortunately she was right in everything she said.

And finally she gave us a piece of good advice,
Never use your own for your flights of fancy.
Instead of a real child, go and get a rag doll,
And with a gentle smile, she threw us out.

The years passed with such merry pranks,
We couldn't imagine getting old,
But we must remember the bad things too,
For most of our lives were taken away.

In '33 there were 33 of us in the class,
Sometimes in jolly mood, we played tricks on each other,
We were brimming with our belief in life,
And this was the year Hitler became ruler of the world.
Our classmates went this way or that,
Some to the right and some to the left.

Difficult and ugly years were to follow. I won't go into detail,
They happened and they passed and I accept the fact.
I do not know anything about what happened to the others,
I hope I will run into one or two sometime.

The world was split in two and we both survived.
You went West, while I am here in the East.
You made a name for yourself, you are a famous man in London.
I can't complain myself, I have no worries.
Sadly we can no longer talk of a common fate,
For a long time we have lived in separate worlds.

When I wrote this letter last night,
I imagined I was inviting you to beautiful Budapest.
Snapshots of Budapest: City Park, Margaret Island,
Hüvösvölgy and Zugliget, you can surely never be forgotten,
János Hill and its sisters Szabadság and Gellért,
Every tourist climbs up them.

The Basilica, Matthias Church, none more beautiful,
A breathtaking view walking along the Fishermen's Bastion.
Váci Street, Andrássy Avenue, the shopping district,
Quality for sale in the capital.

Buildings on the Danube embankment are well maintained,
And since we are here, let's drop into the Hangli.
Busy traffic along Rákóczi Street,
And much merriment in the side streets.
At the Western Railway Station, the future is bright,
When the government district is built, it will be elegant.

Up on top of Castle Hill, there is a beautiful palace,
Kings once lived there, now it is a library.
The journey is convenient, transport by cable car,
And the Sándor Palace is exactly opposite.

Situated in Castle Hill is the Buda tunnel,
The beautiful Chain Bridge practically runs into it.
We'll have a look at the zoo and the funfair today,
Tomorrow we'll visit Vajdahunyad Castle.
The bells of the Jáki Chapel call us to vespers,
No silence in the neighbouring garden restaurant.

A pleasure boat floats quietly on the Danube,
Dark clouds trail in front of the moon.
This doesn't mean rain, the captain reassures me,
But as we near the harbour, our journey is coming to a close.

These were a few sights in Budapest,
It is a very beautiful city, that is undeniable.
There could be improvements of course,
But that will be a task for our children.

Waltzing in the Shadow of Fascism

PAUL FABRY

The long, warm summer months of 1937 were full of promise for the wealthy bourgeoisie in Budapest. They were enjoying their charmed Victorian world of tree-lined promenades along the banks of the Danube. Gypsy bands played waltzes in the elegant cafes for the slow-moving crowd passing by on the Corso. In the middle of a square stood a monument to this happy time – a remnant of the optimistic Austro-Hungarian era – the Hangli restaurant. The shining, tent-like glass structure stood in front of one of the city's famous concert halls. It turned into an upscale nightclub when the sun set over the Buda hills, looking across the river to the illuminated Royal Palace and the churches presenting their spectacular profile at dusk. The Hangli was one of the Ronay family's proud establishments. Just the place to sip your first glass of champagne, served by waiters in white gloves, before the start of the evening's musical performances.

Nearby, the flagship of the Ronays' far-flung business, the ornate Belvárosi Cafe, was collecting petty cash from the card-playing political insiders for their afternoon drinks, making room for the more profitable dinner business to follow. This stylish cafe, with its dark velvet curtains, marble columns and street tables, was situated near a major bridge and at the end of the best shopping street. It was where Egon, already married and with a law degree, could confidently be found in the early evening by his friends.

In the back of the huge restaurant, a narrow corridor and a few steps led to a small and messy office space that served as his headquarters. The elegant heir to the restaurant chain was always ready for a drink, preferably something called a 'Sidecar' (orange liqueur with lemon juice and brandy). An incurable anglophile, Egon invariably had a London paper or magazine on the table nearby. As often as not it would provoke a political conversation. Our younger crowd were already aware of the increasing influence of Hitler and his inflammatory propaganda.

This was when I met Egon. In retrospect we were living the high life that couldn't last, waltzing in the shadow of fascism. A good portion of Budapest society and the majority of its intellectual and artistic leaders had been of Jewish background. Many families had at least one Jewish relative to worry about when Hitler's army arrived later in the war. But it was difficult to be seriously scared at this point, particularly when there was so much good French champagne left in the cellar. The issue of the Ronay family's Jewish ancestry was not discussed. Indeed, during our friendship, which lasted until his death, the subject never came up between us.

Egon's first wife, a beautiful Budapest high-society star, Edith, represented the carefree era's best features. Their elegant apartment in Semmelweis Street was a meeting place for some of the top artists of the capital. But the problems of war and Hitler's demands on Hungary finally had to be addressed. As the summer turned to fall, Egon and I had to move into the Bercsényi barracks of the mounted artillery regiment. High life came to a sudden end for both of us. Except that Egon, to the envy of the rest of us, arrived characteristically well-prepared – with a shiny new car, two Anglo-Arab horses, well-tailored uniforms and a paid 'csicskas' (a peasant boy recruited to serve the officer candidates).

Here we were locked up for a year preparing to fight unknown enemies with outdated artillery equipment and beautiful horses. Egon and other friends, ranging from aristocrats to future victims of the Holocaust, took the army life with resignation. It was the price we paid for being society's golden generation whose rank and doctoral degrees assured status and success. On our days off we ran to the Belvárosi Cafe for a glass of champagne and news of the world.

Egon ironically referred to this Kafkaesque year in nonsensical cavalry-type military service as our 'heroic period' during the next seven decades of correspondence (in three languages) that followed. In my New Orleans filing cabinet I have the thick file of our letters, along with the articles and photographs which are among my key memorabilia of the past century. Perhaps his daughters, Esther and Edina, will one day find them amusing.

In a glass case near the dusty old files there are several silver cigarette cases. They are of the type that were fashionable as gifts to your seconds in a duel between university buddies before the war. Among them there is one given to me by Egon. The inscription engraved inside in

Hungarian says in a particularly warm tone thanks for friendship and is dated Christmas 1944. It was given not as a souvenir for a juvenile duel, but in appreciation for the falsified military documents and birth certificates that we provided for him and some family members in that *annus horribilis*. The reason for the papers' need was never discussed, but I know they sealed our relationship for life.

Egon successfully terminated his year's service in army uniform while I went on to 'liberate the world from Communism' on the Russian front with only periodic visits home. Still, we kept up and met at – where else? – the Belvárosi, with other friends who, one by one, turned against the German string-pullers of Hungary's puppet government.

The gilded lifestyle slowly but surely faded out of a still untouched capital city, but news kept coming in of the horrors of war on the Eastern Front, where a number of Egon's school chums died in army units or labour camps. Hiding in Budapest was increasingly dangerous as fascist police and hateful neighbours turned on anyone with Jewish connections. The final countdown came with the actual German occupation of much of Hungary and the installation of a murderous government that was willing to carry out the cruellest stage of the Holocaust in the autumn of 1944. The elite officers of the army, the leaders of a resistance that could not act in time, were arrested, as were many of Egon's friends.

One of the early chapters of the anti-fascist resistance movement, mostly the intellectuals and some disenchanted officers, used to meet at the Belvárosi. There, at a corner table, Joska, our reliable waiter, would on special occasions serve us precious, room-temperature champagne stored secretly in Egon's back-office cabinet (see page 14 for photo of Joska). Egon moved around the countryside and remained a clandestine participant to the end, as did Peter Zerkovitz, his friend who provided a secret apartment a couple of floors above the cafe for those hiding from the Gestapo. After the mass deportations and killings of this last, terrible phase of the Holocaust played out in the streets and the ghetto of Budapest, Christmas finally signalled the end of the war. At least it did for one half of our devastated, burned out, hungry city. The Soviet Army arrived in the eastern suburbs of Budapest. The Germans were still fighting in the Buda hills, moving back slowly towards Vienna. The Hungarian fascists retreated with them.

We somehow met once more for a champagne toast, by candlelight at Semmelweis Street. Edith managed to decorate a branch of a pine tree with the traditional 'salon-candy' to signify Christmas. The sounds of artillery from both the Russians and Germans crossed the bloody Danube. Dead horses remained in the snow of the boulevards long after dead bodies of people had been pulled into doorways by passers-by.

Egon's lovely engraved silver cigarette case remains a symbol of that Christmas and of our survival. It is a metaphor for a profound change in our lives. This was the end of everything we and our families had known. We had no clue what the future held for us. He often referred to those appalling times when celebrating one or other of his many ambitious projects later in London. It was an essential element of the pride he felt in going on to make an international name for himself.

As is related in this book, Egon loved to tell of how he remarkably opened up as a restaurateur once more in the ruined city, with a coffee-stand for citizens and Russian soldiers alike on the corner of the Belvárosi. He put a hand-painted 'we are open' sign over the broken windows of the cafe that had been his father's since 1910. And Edith resumed her social parties at their apartment whenever electricity and water were available.

In one of his books in London, he wrote about an even more difficult job he faced when I asked him a few months later to organise the new democratic government's first state dinner for Marshal Voroshilov, commander of the Allied Control Commission in Budapest (Nick Ross refers to this). As the cabinet chief of President Tildy, I had to come up with a formal menu and service in the presidential palace when there was hardly any power or transportation available. On top of this, we were told that Stalin's son would be there with the Ambassadors of France, Britain and the US. Egon pulled off an elaborate French dinner with the best wines and white-gloved service, a miracle to all. In his toast, the Marshal, who became the USSR's next president, praised Hungarian cuisine, not realising that most of the ingredients were smuggled in from abroad by his own soldiers who had been bribed by Egon.

By 1946 the political situation in Hungary had become dismal. The classic restaurants and cafes of the Ronay family could not offer an acceptable future for Egon – the Soviets requisitioned Ronay senior's properties, leaving him penniless. All of us, seeing the ruthless rapacity of the Soviets, had only one answer: go west, if at all possible. Egon's many friends had left for America, others moved to South America and Australia. By the time I had resigned my diplomatic post in Turkey in June 1947, he was already urging me to join him in London: come and we can work together… England was indeed the logical place for him to settle given his ability to speak English and his pre-war visits.

On my eventual way to America I stayed with him and Edith in their small London apartment – during a cold winter stretch in 1949. He was already full of new ideas and optimism. This gift never left him; in his nineties he would still call me on the phone with lengthy pitches for new projects, offering me a minor part in one scheme or another, asserting how tough the food business was and how little I knew of it. This was certainly true, as was my conviction of the difficulties there would be in working with someone as stubborn and self-assured as my very dear friend.

There were plans to start a universal 'airguide' together when the airline industry's food services were in their infancy. There was the idea of organising an international wine classification system (long before Parker). Then there was the Académie Internationale de Gastronomie with new chapters to open in America. The festive dinners, from the Bristol in Paris to the Dorchester in London, the openings of elegant clubs based in the spreading World Trade Centers across dozens of cities. A bloody pig-killing festival in communist Hungary – Egon organised it with a cousin of mine in Budapest, George Barandy, just to prove our traditions are not allowed to disappear. A carnival dinner in New Orleans and parties at my home where we spent nights reliving the tough times, only to conclude that there's one universal panacea, the one that always lubricated our countless reunions: fine champagne to wash away all unpleasant memories.

Return to Hungary? It was politically impossible for us during the murderous Rakosi regime. There was a slight thaw by the 1960's and our mutual friends invited us to Budapest to see what remained of our old lives. Egon was reluctant. His good friend, the London bureau chief of *The New York Times*, Johnny Apple, joined me in urging him to go.

Months went by with planning.

Finally we both agreed to catch the same flight from Zurich to Budapest. But the cruel treatment of his family, by both the Nazis and now the Communists, preoccupied him, as did the fate of their family properties and the state of his favourite cafes, and finally the thought of his beloved parents, now in a cemetery he had never visited. At the departure gate I was told that the passenger next to me had not turned up. It was Egon. The flight had to leave. Calls to London and on the loudspeaker followed. Egon was nearby but hesitating in some waiting room, unable to decide. I finally persuaded him to board.

I held his hand all the way to Budapest. On busy Váci Street, near the Belvárosi, he broke down crying, "Even my old school is gone". And the cemetery, and the Hangli, where a Russian statue replaced the famed restaurant. And the dead friends. We ended up for lunch in a run-down Italian trattoria on the site of the former Corso. No gypsy musicians, no elegant strollers, not even the usual prostitutes, he remarked. Then an elderly waiter approached. He stopped short at our table and exclaimed with joy, "You came home, Mr Ronay!" It was good old Joska from the Belvárosi. He knew the ritual and produced a warm bottle of champagne. All was in order. "If you stay everything will be good again," he assured Egon. *Plus ça change, plus c'est la même chose.*

After a heart attack in the 1980's, Egon started reverting to our common mother tongue on the phone. His language ability was phenomenal. Avoiding accents in English, French or German, his vocabulary was as rich as his encyclopedic knowledge of food and wine. He suddenly started addressing me as Captain Gombos, my pseudonym during the years of the Resistance. His Hungarian remained faultless and colourful with old jokes and the endless stories of his parents. He had been an only child and the lost, private world of his family belonged to him alone.

The definitive memoir of his life will never come, because there was nothing definitive or predictable in the 90-plus years we both spent wandering around in search of civilised ways and people. Egon's many friends loved him and thousands admired him around the world. I know he felt very close to me, as I felt about him. Such friendship we both considered the true essence of a meaningful life. A toast to that!

When my wife and I flew into Heathrow the last time to stay with Egon and Barbara in the 1990's, the immigration official asked us why we had come to England. "We are visiting Mr Egon Ronay in Yattendon," we said, which brought suspicious looks and the statement: "Egon Ronay is not a person, it is an institution!" So it is. He is and will remain for those who knew him an institution of good taste and living, an emblematic symbol of a Central European instinct for survival and an unparalleled keeper of a classic heritage that has now passed – let's call it the essence of the 20th century.

How to Become a Restaurant Inspector

Antonio Bolza

On the 22nd of June, 2010 we gathered at the lovely old church of Yattendon in Berkshire for Egon Ronay's funeral. Egon's old friend Dante Campailla told us what an outstanding person Egon was and what his great achievements had been. When the coffin was lowered into its final resting place in that ancient graveyard there was an unexpected disturbance. From a yew tree, towering high into the sky immediately behind the grave, a wood pigeon started up with loudly flapping wings – an omen for me although unnoticed by most. A notable spirit was departing that day. Many of his old friends met again a few months later at a Dorchester dinner to pay tribute to Egon. I was permitted to say a few words. This gave me the chance to articulate my gratitude to Egon – it was he who had started me off in my career and I owe him a lot.

I first met Egon in Vienna in 1965; I was 21 years old. Egon interviewed me for a temporary job as an inspector for his Ski Guide. I got the job of reporting on many of the Austrian resorts, provided I could get hold of a car. My dear mother willingly lent me her only car, an ancient VW-Beetle, so I could take on the job, my first ever. The trusty car did not let me down. With its studded back tyres I never once got stuck in the Alpine snow, even crossing the Arlberg Pass and overtaking many much grander cars, immobilised until they could fit their snow chains. It was not an easy job travelling, checking in, inspecting the runs, assessing the hotels, tasting the nightlife and talking to the local tourist office – and, most importantly, hacking away for hours at night on the small portable Olivetti typewriter my (secret) fiancée had given me to use. Reports in English, of course; no spellcheck, no changing of words, but two carbon copies for each report in case one went astray. Posting my daily reports to London I got to know all the post offices in the Alps intimately. I finished as planned three months later having had just one weekend off. The job was over, so I thought. But I was just grateful to have had the assignment at all. I had been an utter failure at school due to dyslexia – unknown and undiagnosed in those days.

I was hanging around back in Vienna a few weeks later when one evening the phone rang. It was Egon. A call from London was something special in 1966. "Why have you not answered my letter? I offered you a job here in England because you did so well on the *Ski Guide*." This was unmistakably Egon's irritated voice over the crackling line. His letter had never arrived, of course. But I seemed to be forgiven because a few days later I found myself with my one and only cardboard suitcase containing all my belongings on a BA Trident flight to Heathrow – my first flight ever. I did, indeed, desperately need a job. But the real reason

I took off on this scary flight was that my (by then not so secret) fiancée was due to be removed by her parents from Vienna to Brussels as far away as possible from the hopeless-Hungarian-refugee-with-no-future whom she had fallen in love with. I hated geography at school because I could not keep all these names in my head, but one thing I did know was that London and Brussels were only separated by a bit of water – easy to cross.

Geza Luby, Egon's director (Hungarian too), who had to my delight known some of my family members back in Budapest, whisked me away briefly to Gravetye Manor in Sussex. I was still pale and trembling from the flight and from there it was straight on to a three-star Spanish restaurant near Ascot. Strangely, the menu was in French, of which I did not speak a word. The waiter came and in desperation I pointed at an unpronounceable name right in the middle of their elaborate card. What arrived was a huge plate of yellow rice covered with animals giving off, as I thought, a rather nasty smell of burnt fingernails mixed with fish. It was a seafood paella, something I had never encountered before. Although I had not eaten since my early breakfast in Vienna, I did not touch it, pretending still to be sick from the flight. Early the following morning we met in the lobby to pay the bill. Then I was told we were off to see the manager back at Gravetye Manor. By this time it was around 9 am and I was famished. I dared to ask Geza about that famous English breakfast I had heard of in school. "Didn't you test the room service?" I had no idea such a thing existed. Too late, the manager appeared to show us around. I was quite ravenous by this time and would probably have eaten even that pungent yellow rice, if offered.

Some days later I was adopted by Major Donald Gray, Egon's most senior inspector. He had lost his left eye in the war and I was impressed by his black eye patch and even more by the glass eye he popped in for driving – so that the police would not know he was handicapped (see page 15 for photo of Gray). I had to get used to many things, like being driven on the left and being carsick when not behind the wheel. I was impressed by the many neat-looking pubs we passed in Somerset and by the friendliness of the people when one asked for directions. I was less impressed by the stewed Cona coffee bubbling away all day and was convinced it was just coloured water with some strange flavour added. I was particularly charmed that I could call someone like Major Gray simply by his name, Donald, when in Austria addressing him as nothing less than 'Major Gray' would have been obligatory.

Donald was a very kind and considerate gentleman and taught me a great deal. I found it quite easy to write about the hotels we inspected and to get the percentage for the grading right, but I struggled considerably with the food, the sauces and the wines. After all, I was a provincial boy when Egon took me on. Following three months on the road with Donald I got my further training at Le Meurice in Paris and the Savoy in London, having managed to bluff my way up to that stage. I passed the test and became an inspector of the Egon Ronay Organisation. I earned £100 a month – my first proper salary.

How proud I was when I fetched my rented Mini from somewhere in north London to drive off on my own, aiming for the famous The Hole in the Wall near Bath at the start of my first tour of the West Country. My good, instinctive sense of direction had always depended on the position of the sun in the sky. But this was England – there was no sun. I spent the first four hours driving round in circles in London

– I had no idea how vast the capital city was. I stopped my Mini many times asking for directions to Bath, finding myself stranded somewhere in Shepherd's Bush more than once. Even the reserved Englishmen showed strong signs of disbelief. One even suggested I buy a map, a good idea, of course, but I had never liked reading maps. I somehow finally escaped the metropolis and made it in time for dinner and felt great. This called for a pre-dinner Campari Soda as a reward (but always remembering that we had to pay for personal drinks ourselves – a strict Ronay rule).

Weeks later, at the Imperial Hotel in Torquay, my family's past caught up with me most unexpectedly. Having arrived on my own in that Mini and carrying just a single cardboard suitcase, I must have raised some eyebrows with the experienced doorman. I probably even blushed when checking in. Their restaurant in those days had three Egon Ronay stars and I was nervous having to eat there on my own. Once ordered, with the first course consumed, the manager appeared. "Is everything all right, sir?" Yes, thank you – I was praying he would leave me alone. He came back after the main course and asked the same question. With the delicious dessert in front of me and begging to be eaten, he was back again for another chat. I almost choked with nervousness. "Excuse me, sir, for interrupting you again, but would you mind me asking two personal questions? The first is not important to me, but I assume you are working for Egon Ronay? The second one is why I came to your table three times. I read your rather rare name in the registry. Do you know of some relations of yours living in Pressburg before the First World War, having three children named Geza, Ilona and Antal?" "Yes, I do", I replied with shaking voice, "Antal would be my father". Pressburg, now Bratislava, is where my family came from.

Without a further word the manager, who turned out also to be the owner, grabbed my arm, pulled me up from my chair and away from my highly desired dessert, dragged me out of the dining room, out of the hotel, into his car and up to his private house. He mumbled, with tears in his eyes, something like, "Sorry, but I can't explain now, I have to take you straight to my home to meet someone". This someone turned out to be a Czech lady and my father's former nanny, now in her late eighties. Mazzi was her name. I realised I remembered mention of her from the stories I had heard my father tell. Just after the First World War, when my father was four, she had left my grandparents' employ to work for another Pressburg family by the name of Von Prueger, now Chapman. They had later moved with her to Britain. Forty-seven years after bidding farewell to my father, his nanny was meeting his son, aged 22! It was a crying match – and what a coincidence. We called my father and he still remembered her well. It was a timely encounter as she then died the following year.

Dramas were frequent on the road. In Aylesbury I got thrown out of a starred restaurant by the owner when testing his famous duck. The meat was white and I complained it was chicken and not a duckling. My way of thinking was they were cheating and saving money. "Sir, be so kind as to get up from this table and leave my restaurant immediately." And this was not said sotto voce – the entire restaurant was listening! Back in Austria the only duck I had ever eaten was wild duck – and it does have dark meat. It was not until 40 years later I told that story to Egon. We were having a memorable luncheon at Tom Aikens in London with his wife, Barbara, and my wife, Angelika, in 2005 shortly before he turned 90. As I recounted my faux pas Egon's laughter rang out across the restaurant.

In 1967 my trans-Channel relationship had blossomed further and I planned to get married. I could not continue as a travelling taster and I needed to earn more. I guessed I would need to move on, but how to tell Egon? I plucked up courage at the end of my inspection tour and explained my predicament. It was nervewracking since he radiated great authority and commanded huge respect. Here was this young man of just 23 years delivering an ultimatum, and straight after having been trained by the organisation. Egon's intense grey eyes seemed to penetrate my very soul as he listened to my plea. But in the end I discovered he wanted to keep me. So I was offered an office job and promotion to Assistant Administrative Manager, plus a salary increase – my final, desperate demand. By the time I got married, the same year, I had proudly saved a little over £1,000 – a small fortune for me.

Egon continued to be more than generous to me. Let me give you an example: not long after we married my wife had a miscarriage. She was visiting her parents in Austria at the time while I was back in London. Because I was alone Egon asked me to spend a weekend with him and Barbara at their new home in Walton Street, taking me out for dinner to San Lorenzo in Beauchamp Place. I was miserable and I must have been terrible company. The very next morning Egon had bought me an airline ticket, reuniting me with my wife for a few days. I often think about that, for today we happen to own a pied-à-terre in Walton Street, close by Egon's former house.

One morning Egon took me to Wilton's for a drink before lunch, just the two of us, as a reward for some good idea I must have had.

He ordered two glasses of Champagne and half a dozen oysters each. I got that first slimy beast down with a large swig of my Champagne and negotiated the second with equal gusto. Suddenly I found I was sweating and choking and my face had apparently gone deep purple. I was having an extreme allergic reaction. I grabbed my glass hoping a swig of Champagne might soothe me but there was none left in my glass. Gradually my turbulence seemed to subside and Egon seized the initiative. He immediately ordered me some langoustines instead. I had already learned to love them on the road and lunch was resumed without further embarrassment. I regularly go to Wilton's even today and I always order langoustines. But I have never ever touched an oyster again.

Young men are restless and in due course it really was time to move on. I finally left ERO in February 1970, a full four years after landing at Heathrow. And I departed with a Yorkshire Terrier puppy in my arms, the charming leaving present given me by the office staff. After I left Egon I went into publishing in Munich, ending up with my own group producing art books and encyclopedias. I had stayed in touch with Egon and one evening, some ten years later, he called me, adopting that reserved tone we all knew. He was clearly hatching some plan or other. To further it he wanted to meet me in London for lunch on my next visit. When we got together he came out with it. He asked me to take over the Egon Ronay Organisation. He would transfer it to me for free as long as I promised to continue to run the business in the same spirit as he always had. I was very flattered but unfortunately had to decline. I had, by this time, built up my own business and constructed a family house on a Bavarian lake. And talking of family – we now had five children and we didn't feel it would be right to uproot them. It was a sad moment for us both, but what a great gesture and amazing honour it was for me.

In 1994 I sold my business and moved to Italy to do something quite different. I purchased the large but decaying estate of Castello di Reschio in Umbria. Egon and Barbara, with a group of friends in tow, visited us a year later when we had just started the vast job of developing the estate. My vision for the place must have sounded like an impossible dream. But it was Egon who once again had confidence in me, strongly encouraging me to go for it. And he was right again too. I owe a great deal of my self-esteem to Egon. My life and my destiny ever since 1965 remained closely interwoven with him. Nobody had believed in me before him. He thought he saw something in me and he trusted his judgement, employing a young man from Austria. He gave me my very first chance in life, he trained me and he taught me how to lead an organisation by his own example. I recall that I also dared to disagree with him on several occasions. I guess these confrontations only served to strengthen our relationship.

Let me shed one more shaft of light on Egon Ronay: an indelible memory I have of him. In his unpretentious office in Queen's House on Leicester Square this short man had built a podium for his imposing table and chair. The visitors found themselves looking up at the master behind his desk. They were on a lower level, as any supplicant should be, with Egon looking down on them. Even when standing we found that his head was triumphantly level with ours. I am sure that today Egon once again looks down on us from somewhere high up with the same air of triumph, with the same little smile on his face and that same knowing sparkle in his ever searching eyes. I am proud of having known Egon for 45 years, I am proud to have been his pupil and I am proud to have led my life without disappointing him.

A Hungarian Brit or a
British Hungarian?

Peter Bazalgette

Egon Ronay spent 31 years of his long life in Hungary and 63 years in Britain, voting in elections and carrying a UK passport. So did that make him more British than Hungarian? Those who knew him well would say, at his core, he remained a proud Hungarian. But the story is more complicated than that. He was educated as a Catholic and, as we learn elsewhere in this book, had Jewish blood. Egon's grandfather, as well as his father, was a hotelier – it was not unusual for Jewish families to be in the hospitality business in Central Europe. His experiences growing up in the 1920's and 1930's will have influenced his attitudes and outlook. Egon's daughter Esther says that he had been "mocked as a Jew" at school. I don't want to over-emphasise this influence, but anti-Semitism grew as a force throughout the 1930's. The father of Egon's first wife, Edith, forbade the marriage because he did not want someone he took to be a Jew marrying into his Catholic family. And, as Nick Ross explains in his chapter, Egon later had to rescue his uncle from a Nazi internment camp in 1944.

What's my point? Merely, that as well as being a member of a well-to-do, middle class, Hungarian family, there were experiences that gave Egon Ronay the sensibility of an outsider, both when he lived in Hungary and certainly after he settled in England. I believe this partly explains his resolute campaigning, and his taking on of the establishment. Of course we all know that he enjoyed publicity, and that his campaigns helped sell his guidebooks. We also know that the standard of public food in Britain was disgraceful, and that these crusades were therefore highly justified. But there was more to it than that. Egon Ronay learnt to deal with, and when necessary, take on the established order from an early age and his life's achievements suggest a complex set of motives.

Why did Egon come to Britain in 1946 rather than the United States, like his friend, Paul Fabry, a contributor to this book? Many Hungarians came here before, during and after the war, from the economist Lord Balogh to the author of *How To Be An Alien*, George Mikes. But there were already many connections between Britain and Egon Ronay in the first third of his life that would point to his eventual destination. The first was that most fashionable of accessories amongst the Austro-Hungarian middle class: an English nanny. Egon left a fragment of autobiography – 1,600 words covering a few of his earliest memories – and his daughter, Edina, has shown it to me. One passage, redolent of *Emile and the Detectives*, recalls how, in 1922 at the age of seven, he apprehended a burglar in the family apartment:

Rooted to the floor and frozen with fear I waited until my governess came to see what kept me.

"There is a strange man here," I said.

The resolute Miss Petrey, who was English, grabbed my hand, dragged me quickly to my room, which was hers too, and checked whether her purse was intact. It was, and we ran out of the flat in a panic leaving the burglar to escape.

Miss Petrey then hurried down four long flights of stairs, pulling me with her, and we rushed to Uncle John down the side street. We didn't have a telephone and his bistro was so near we could see it from our window. A reassuringly burly, well-built man with a billiard-ball head and a cropped moustache, my mother's brother-in-law was a natural choice when in physical danger. He rushed us back to the apartment house, summoning a policeman on the way. All policemen were just as burly as my uncle and wore long swords hanging from their waist.

Now Miss Petrey and I ran back home in the wake of the two giants. The concierge, who kept the key to the lift, was called and we hastened back up to the flat, where all the rooms were thoroughly examined, my uncle leading the search. In my parents' bedroom the policeman drew his sword and swung it to and fro under the bed and thrust it under and over the mattress, with no success.

Later, Egon recounts, he is asked to identify the miscreant but declined to do so. In retrospect this baffled him because, "I must have had the killer instinct, without which it wouldn't have been possible to survive the three apocalyptic decades that were to follow".

Having come under the, no doubt, formidable influence of Miss

Petrey, Egon was then sent to Britain to improve his English. In his mid-teens he stayed with a family in Kent where he developed a powerful crush on the daughter of the household – a memory that came back to him intensely in old age. His personal photo-album from the 1930's has many pages of black and white snaps of people he befriended as well as the usual tourist sites – Buckingham Palace, the Palace of Westminster and so on. Later, when a law student in Budapest, he attended English language summer schools in Cambridge. At this time he became close friends with Eric Baker (and later set up home at Longfield in Kent to be near him). He also got an internship at a London hotel. His growing affection for England is exemplified by his application, in the mid-1930's, to study postgraduate law at Trinity Hall, Cambridge. He was interviewed and offered a place but decided in the end to stay and assist his father with the family business. This was a decision expected of him as his father was unwell and Egon was an only child.

At his Cambridge interview Egon was guided around the college and he expressed astonishment when shown the memorial to members who had died in the First World War. German alumni were commemorated alongside the British who had fallen. In Egon's black and white world it was always clear who was on which side. I remember him being equally amazed when, at a party of mine, he met the editor of a magazine that had published an extremely unflattering review of a book I had written: "How could you invite him ?" He was, indeed, a duellist by nature.

So it was to London Egon fled in 1946. His wife, Edith, joined him shortly afterwards and his two daughters followed by train in 1947, shepherded by their maternal grandmother. One of them, Edina, says it was very hard to start with nothing, especially after the glamorous life they had enjoyed in pre-war Budapest. But she remembers how ecstatic her father was when they all received their naturalisation papers, becoming British citizens.

Egon was never to see his father again. Edina explained to me how tough this was for the family. "After communism had set in firmly he could no longer go back to Budapest and neither could his parents come to visit us. This was an extremely hard blow for him. The only time I ever saw him cry was when he received the news that his father had died." Edina's sister, Esther, also recalls the hardship of separation and the shock in the family when they heard that Egon's mother had died and that her jewellery had been stolen from her body immediately afterwards. This is how it was for an only child starting a new life in another country.

Armed with introductions into the hospitality business Egon quickly secured the job of general manager for The Society Restaurant in Jermyn Street (later the site became the nightclub Tramp). Egon described the Society as, "a beautiful, wood-panelled dining room, sophisticated, elegant and frequented by the cream of society". In his 1989 book, *The Unforgettable Dishes of My Life*, he recalled a particular night:

One day in 1948 or 1949 a table was booked for Princess Margaret and her party. I wanted to do my best to 'dress' the room, as they used to say, with suitable young couples preferably in dinner jackets, but I only had 24 hours in which to do it.

A month earlier an impecunious, 20 year old émigré friend, who came from a very good family and was studying at Manchester University, had asked for my help and a job. All I could offer him was £5 a week to spend eight hours a day in a tiny basement room cleaning the large number of huge, silver candelabra that was a hallmark of the restaurant. But it was to him that I turned in my predicament on the day of the Princess's visit. Did he have a girlfriend? (A superfluous question to ask a Hungarian.) Did he have a dinner jacket and his girlfriend an evening dress? They did. I gave him the afternoon off to get organised and on the dot of 7.30 my dashing and smart silver cleaner, with a ravishing girl on his arm, was received by my head waiter who didn't recognise him (Professor Higgins would have been proud), and placed him, as I instructed, next to where the Princess was due to be seated. Next morning at 8 am sharp he was back in his basement chrysalis from where he had emerged for a royal evening.

After 50 years Egon still recalled that one of the side dishes the Princess dined on was that English classic, bubble and squeak, but with the very Hungarian additions of sour cream and caraway seeds.

In due course this ambitious, intelligent, smartly dressed, immaculately mannered Hungarian immigrant moved on. He agreed to become the stage manager and impresario of a daily gastronomic performance in the West End. He was, of course, perfectly at home in the world of the grand restaurant. Forty years later, in *The Unforgettable Dishes of My Life*, he wrote about this new job:

The ethos and classic tradition of grand restaurants have almost disappeared. The '96 Piccadilly', of which I was a very young general manager in the 1950's, was one. Elevated to fame through a visit by the then Princess Elizabeth, it was a large establishment of many elegant dining rooms. I would receive tout Londres in its lounge and instantly decide whom to sit at which table – an important judgement only to those who did not matter. This was called the art of 'dressing the room', ensuring that easily recognisable VIP's sat where they could be seen instantly from the entrance, flanked by tables with attractive women whoever they may be – a bone of contention with important but older and less attractive women. How absurd it now seems!

In retrospect it is extraordinary how long Egon worked as a manager for other people – the best part of a decade. He did so because he had to. But his independence of mind and entrepreneurial spirit won out in the end and he decided to open his own place. He was his father's son. In 1952 he gathered investors, including a travel agent who was later to die in the famous 'Busby Babes', Manchester United plane crash. And he found a site, a tiny former cafe in Hans Road, down the side of Harrods. It had a forbiddingly high ceiling so it was designed with an apparent drape, in the manner of a marquee. This became its name.

For Egon the critical recruit was the chef and he decided to lure the Frenchman Jean Gardes away from 96 Piccadilly (see page 15 for photo of Gardes). He greatly admired his skill and felt an affinity for him, having originally brought him over from Beaulieu in the South of France. Gardes specialised in French classics such as pâté de campagne, chaud-froid de volaille, omelette gratinée, truite farcie and bouillabaisse. The last was only put on the menu for the following day when well-briefed Cornish fishermen had first contacted Billingsgate to let it be known they had each of the prescribed ten fish and crustacea that chef Gardes regarded as indispensable for an authentic fish stew.

The food scene in post-war London, even by the early 1950's, remained somewhat drab. Rationing was only fully phased out by 1953. But a small band of aficionados were seeking better things, encouraged by Elizabeth David who had by now published *A Book of Mediterranean Food* and *French Country Cooking*. Partly because there were no classic restaurants outside the West End at that time and partly thanks to its proximity to Harrods and its ladies-who-lunch, The Marquee rapidly took off. Its reputation was sealed when Fanny Cradock, then an influential columnist in *The Daily Telegraph*, described it as "London's most food perfect restaurant". Discovering and popularising a new restaurant of merit was something Egon himself was to excel at later on. This time he was on the receiving end and business was brisk:

With all the publicity and being opposite the side entrance of Harrods lunches were particularly hectic, taking orders, seating the influx, running up and down stairs to the kitchen and keeping an eye on the waitresses, I was near collapse. A friend of mine, a known wag, watched me and as he was leaving said: "How much will you pay me if I don't come tomorrow?"

Egon kept a menu from April 15th, 1954 which demonstrates how fashionable The Marquee became. It is signed not only by chef Gardes but by a number of major celebrities of the time, including Lady Isobel Barnett and Gilbert Harding. His famous clientele were not always easy. Gilbert Harding, notoriously cantankerous, accused Egon of serving tinned grapefruit. He could not believe anyone would individually skin segments, but that is exactly what Gardes demanded of his team. On another occasion a lugubrious-looking young man asked, with a tone of injured disappointment, why there was no garlic in his Salade Niçoise.

It was a youthful Clement Freud. As far as Gardes was concerned, garlic could be added to the dish but did not strictly belong in it (and he was from the South of France). Though he regretted it later, Egon turned on the young would-be gastronome and said, "You have a lot to learn". "So have you", fired back Freud and left in a huff.

We tend to believe that today's phenomenon of the celebrity chef is something recent. But Fanny Cradock introduced more than a whiff of show business into the food world at the same time as Egon was establishing himself as a restaurateur. Even before she first appeared on television in 1955 she and her 'husband', Major Johnnie Cradock, would book theatres to perform a sort of food cabaret, feeding the front row with titbits. Sometimes the entire performance would be followed by a panel discussion and, having praised The Marquee in print, she invited Egon to participate. Thus he once found himself in Birmingham, watching Fanny rehearse. Then the man who was to chair the discussion arrived. Egon could not remember who this was but it was a very big broadcasting figure of the time – probably Max Robertson or McDonald Hobley. The chairman strode forward to say hello to Fanny who was concentrating rather hard on the tricky task of stuffing a turkey. She looked up and said, "I'm busy, so kindly fuck off". The broadcaster was so flabbergasted that he turned tail for the first train back to London. Egon was despatched to persuade him back, which he eventually succeeded in doing.

Fanny Cradock may have been an average cook, a bigamist and a pantomime dame with the manners of a fishwife, but Egon owed her a lot. Not only did she celebrate his restaurant and launch him on the stage as a man with opinions about food, she also recommended him as her successor at *The Daily Telegraph* when she moved to *The Daily Mail* in 1955. He took to journalism with enthusiasm, adopting a style and tone all of his own. But he soon found that he could not combine the careers of journalist and restaurateur. Enthused by the new role and exhausted by the old he gave up The Marquee.

In a decade Egon had moved from penniless Hungarian immigrant to celebrated restaurateur and now national newspaper columnist. He had penetrated British society and now he had the means to criticise it. In the years to come that was something he would do with relish.

Egon's task as a regular columnist started out as a straightforward restaurant reviewer. But he quickly broadened it out to include more general culinary issues. And it was influential – *The Daily Telegraph's* circulation in the 1950's was around 1.2 million with a readership of twice that number. And there were only three restaurant review columns in print in Britain. In 1958 Egon decided to collect some of his reviews into a book and 1959 saw the publication of his first, slim guide, covering 175 restaurants in the London area. Its full name was *Egon Ronay recommends 175 eating places in and around London*. The cover of a second edition proudly announces, "First printing sold out in two weeks". In his Introduction Egon tackled two of his favourite themes: the importance of exposing low standards and how diffident Britain's ruling class was when it came to food. Here is an excellent example of both the affectionate exasperation he felt for his adopted country, and the idiosyncratic but effective syntax he employed with his adopted language:

There is only one weapon, the use of which the British public has yet to learn: complaints. Britons do enjoy good food just as much as Continentals do – though this is surprising in view of the scandalously inferior and stupidly spartan feeding, a large section of the better-off are brought up to tolerate at public schools. Consequently they are too shy to say what they really think, even when asked, thereby doing a great disservice to the restaurateur. So, they only have themselves to blame.

Promoted by his column, the new guide sold extremely well. So by the end of the 1950's the restaurateur-cum-journalist had also become a publisher and his eponymous Guides business was born. Before long he had to hire inspectors and he recruited them via his famous annual small ad in the Personal section of *The Times*, as Michael Edwards recalls in his chapter.

Egon soon discovered that a peppery introduction to the Guide made for good PR. He would pen a short essay with judicious observations about the restaurant scene in general, or standards of service in hotels or perhaps the quality of public food, and then whack it out as a press release, the more inflammatory the better. Fleet Street lapped it up. In 1968 and 1970 he condemned no less treasured an institution than the British breakfast. In 1969 hotel chambermaids were dismissed as "strict, sadistic, unkempt and immune to 'do not disturb' notices". 1972 saw a clever survey of hospital catering where Egon persuaded junior hospital doctors to do the inspections. The results were "scandalously low standard" and, in one place, "simply revolting". As these surveys garnered headlines in hundreds of national and local newspapers, the cartoonists got to work – a sure sign of traction in the national consciousness. When Egon's hospital food story was in vogue Jak, the cartoonist in *The Evening Standard*, had a dinner-jacketed old buffer being wheeled into Casualty on a trolley anxiously asking: "Are you sure it's got the Egon Ronay seal of approval?"

In 1977 it was the turn of the catering at Victoria Coach Station: "unpalatable . . . often horrifying food . . . a bad smell . . . dirty . . . litter is strewn everywhere". Then it was food on the cross-Channel ferries in 1981: "lamentable hamburgers, horrid water-logged vegetables, impenetrable fried scampi, cardboard-filled sandwiches". And in 1983 he had two targets, the first of which was food served in West End theatres, summed up as "appalling". A further *Evening Standard* cartoon had a billboard outside a theatre saying, "Appalling Soggy Murky Poor – Egon Ronay" as one theatre-goer was saying to another: "No, that's the restaurant – I believe the play's quite good". Egon also sent an inspector to London Zoo that year where a chair in the cafeteria was so filthy his trousers stuck to it. Marc, the pocket cartoonist in *The Times*, had a posh lady accompanied by a prep school boy asking the zoo attendant: "What time are they feeding the tourists?"

Two of Egon's public food obsessions stand out, because of the number of times he returned to them and because of his prescience as to what the root cause of the problems were. In 1975 he sent his inspectors in to scrutinise the food outlets at Heathrow and Gatwick. At Heathrow they found, "a battered cheese sandwich . . . with an exiguous smear of butter, chewy sponge cake, apple pie with limp pastry . . . double gloucester cheese sweating". Gatwick fared even worse: "absolutely deplorable, dirty with poor food and inept service". Giles, *The Daily Express*'s cartoonist, had a man stopped by airport security complaining that the small dots on the X-ray were not concealed bullets but 'fresh' English garden peas.

Egon observed that one monopoly, The British Airports Authority, was often granting another monopoly to caterers such as Trust House Forte (this was a full 35 years before BAA's monopoly was finally broken up, judged as being against the public interest). In 1982 he had another go at airport catering and then again in 1988 when a bitter legal action ensued between Egon and Charles Forte (see Dante Campailla's chapter – The Lawyer's Lawyer). And if we hadn't been poisoned in the departure lounge, there was always the airline itself to assault our palates. In 1984 Egon sent inspectors (including Simon Hopkinson, later the chef at Hilaire and Bibendum) on to most of the major carriers and the verdict was: "rubbishy food . . . soapy cheddar . . . stewed coffee . . . finger breaking rolls . . . stale bread . . . fat gristly meat".

But the campaign with which Egon was most famously associated, over a period of 50 years, was motorway service stations. From the late 1950's Britain began to construct a motorway network and in 1959 and 1960 Egon wrote a series of articles in *The Daily Telegraph* warning against the approach they were taking to the establishment of the motorway stops – allowing large companies to bid for entire concessions and making no mention of catering standards in the procurement process. He contrasted this with service stations on the Continent, already in operation, where the government kept control of them and allowed family businesses to bid for the catering concessions. This had led to diversity and high standards. He was ignored. So by 1972 he mounted another warning in *The Guardian* that The Department of Transport was still awarding leases without reference to catering standards and expertise. Stung by his repeated criticism, in 1978 the Department announced a Commission of Inquiry. Like most such exercises it was really designed to kick the issue into the long grass – nothing came of it. Egon was filmed for BBC television news at one site attempting to eat a jelly pudding which, while apparently cemented to his spoon at one end, sprung up and down like an elasticated yo-yo. Trust House Forte owned several of the motorway sites and so the animated ping-pong between Sir Charles Forte and Egon intensified as the years went by. Forte told the BBC's Cliff Michelmore that he regularly visited THF's service stations: "I usually order bacon, eggs, chips and coffee. I've yet to be disappointed". On one occasion he wrote to The Times, whose letter page was then Britain's most influential debating forum: "Who is he (Ronay) to say those things? People come from all over the world to look at our motorway operations because they're so good". On another occasion he used *The Times* to accuse Egon of "using emotive words such as awful and appalling . . . undermining tourism . . . and undermining the morale of service station staff".

What was the truth of it? Was Egon applying unfairly high standards to simple fare? Not at all, he just wanted chips, bangers and the rest to be the best they could. Before choice and competition were introduced at these sites, with the multiple concessions we're familiar with today, standards were uniformly dire. The only visible exception was the Tebay Services near Penrith on the M6. Egon garlanded them with awards. And the difference was that this was family owned and they cared about food. It remains one of the best today. Further vindication came for Egon's campaigning when he launched yet another broadside against the service stations via his new website in 2000. Finally one of the largest operators, Welcome Break, then sought Egon's help to improve their services (as, indeed, BAA had done a decade earlier). Welcome

Break's Chief Executive at the time, Richard Pennycook, writes about it in his chapter of this book.

Speaking on Radio 4 not long before his death, Egon agreed there was considerable animosity between him and Forte – both short, unyielding and from immigrant families but with rather different views as to how the British should eat. Egon argued that his campaign was exactly what was wanted at the time. When food is no good he said he always had the same reaction: "I feel literally angry. What the hell's going on here?" And as to why he was so critical by nature – he put that down to the experience of being with his father in 1930's Budapest. In the early evening they would each pick up a spoon and taste their way through the soups and sauces prepared for the evening service. His father always had acute comments to make, both positive and negative. Thus Egon's palate was trained, to which he later added his own campaigning zeal, combative nature and, yes, flair for publicity. The last word on his 50-year struggle against British lethargy and poor cuisine goes to Keith Waterhouse in his *Daily Mirror* column in 1983:

> *As regular a feature of the English spring as the first cuckoo and the clocks being put forward is the sound of Egon Ronay going "Bleah". This is inevitably followed by the sharp chirrup-chirrup of a dawn chorus of restaurant managers protesting: "Mr Ronay is being most unfair when he describes our food as being not fit to put before pigs. We had a party of pigs in only the night before last and they had very few complaints."*

While Ronay Guides dished out brickbats to public catering every year, its serious purpose was to discover, encourage and celebrate good cooking in restaurants, hotels and pubs. Chefs as diverse as Rick Stein, Marco Pierre White, Simon Hopkinson, Pierre Koffmann, Joyce Molyneux, and Raymond Blanc were all spotted early on by Egon's inspectors and then lauded and publicised. So when the 23-year-old former French waiter Raymond Blanc opened a tiny restaurant in a shopping arcade in Oxford's Summertown, word soon got to Egon. Blanc was made restaurateur of the year in 1978 and it was life-changing: "I was told – we have Egon Ronay in tonight. I said who? But it changed my life in many ways. It filled up my restaurant, kept it open and saved my life." Pierre Koffmann has arguably been the finest chef in London in the last 30 years. He cooked at The Waterside Inn at Bray and later at his own La Tante Claire in Chelsea: "He was a gentleman. He preferred chefs who were working in their kitchens rather than on TV. In the old days critics could fill up or empty a restaurant. I was lucky to have a good report! I respected him and was always pleased to see him."

In 2001 I witnessed at first hand his extraordinary enthusiasm for culinary discoveries. Egon was staying with my wife and me in south Devon and we took him to a tiny fish restaurant near Bigbury called The Oyster Shack. The owners ran an oyster farm in the Bantham estuary and they had tacked on a sort of cafe in which you could consume their oysters with a limited range of smoked fish, bringing your own white Burgundy along to enhance the experience. Egon liked it and insisted on interviewing the owner at great length. He set out to know all about oyster farming and, having discovered all its secrets, then publicised the surprised owners on his personal website. He wanted them to succeed and he wanted others to enjoy the experience.

Grete Hobbs and her husband Joe inherited Inverlochy Castle near Fort William in the Scottish Highlands. Joe's father had owned the Ben Nevis whisky distillery and bought and restored the nearby castle after the war. The Hobbses lived in Leicestershire and simply used it in the school holidays. But they soon found they could not afford its upkeep. Someone suggested they take in paying guests and, once they had persuaded their cook to feed the clientele, they opened up. This is how Grete remembers it:

Mary Shaw was a Gaelic speaker from the Isle of Harris. In my opinion she was the best cook in Britain. We had to beg her to stay on. But we were complete amateurs when we started off – it was our home. Not long after that a young man arrived in a tiny car. I was suspicious of him – he looked like the sort who would do a flit in the night. So I parked my car behind his to block it in. He scoffed everything and at the end presented a card saying he was an Egon Ronay inspector. I'd never heard of Egon Ronay. How they ever found us I'll never know. Then another older inspector came. Two months after a very smart, short gentleman came in with a younger man. We only found out it was Egon Ronay because he had an advanced driving licence on the windscreen of his Jaguar carrying his name. He later wrote and said he wanted to give us a special mention because he thought Mary's cooking was so good. He had two criticisms which, he said, if we tackled he would make us hotel of the year. He said the bath towels were too small and the wine list was not good enough. I went straight to Harrods to buy the biggest towels I could find and I got Avery's of Bristol in to help with a new wine list. We were 1971 Hotel of the Year and we took off. There's no doubt he had an enormous effect on

Inverlochy. He discovered it, he started us off. If he hadn't I don't know what would have happened to us.

Inverlochy Castle remains a premier hotel today, long after Grete Hobbs has retired from running it. Another restaurant still going strong, more than thirty years after the Ronay Guide singled it out, is McCoys at the Tontine in North Yorkshire. The three McCoy brothers, whose parents were publicans, ran a nightclub on Teesside where the likes of Rod Stewart, Jimi Hendrix and The Rolling Stones all performed. They then started an eccentric bistro in a disused basement of the club. Word of this reached the Ronay Organisation and Eugene McCoy remembers clearly what happened next:

One night I arrived at the restaurant at 6.45 pm in the pouring rain to open up. Already there was a solitary man in a long overcoat waiting outside. I thought – does he want money? Anyway, we put him in the bar to dry out. He had dinner including our chicken satay dish. He shook my hand on the way out and said, "One day you'll be as famous as The Box Tree" (the celebrated restaurant in Ilkley). Not long afterwards Egon Ronay and a colleague visited us. They had lots to eat with half a bottle of Krug beforehand, a 1969 Puligny Montrachet and, I remember, it was a 1965 Château Climens to finish. Afterwards he asked us to sit with him and he said, "I'd like to make your restaurant very famous". We said, "You can't, we're moving in six months". Egon said, "You can't, I don't believe this – you can't move!" We insisted we were, so he asked us to let him know when we were open again in the new place.

Eighteen months later we were inspected twice, though we didn't know it at the time. Then Egon sent us a telegram to say we'd be Restaurant of the Year for 1979. He sent Quentin Crewe who wrote five pages about us in The Sunday Times. *He even sent Johnny Apple from* The New York Times. *The business went mad – it went berserk. It was quite fantastic. From 15 or 20 a night we were full with 60 and turning more away. A black Mercedes turned up with six posh ladies from Leeds who demanded a table and got quite abusive when I insisted we were booked out. One couple flew from California.*

We sent Egon a telegram back with huge thanks and we added ironically, "Why did you destroy our backwater happiness?" He liked that. When we met he always asked how our backwater happiness was going. Egon Ronay had a massive effect on British eating out. He made people realise what good food is. He wanted standards to get better and they did.

In 1977 a 16-year-old youth called Marco White came down to London from Yorkshire. He'd already worked at The Box Tree in Ilkley and went on to cook for the Roux brothers, Pierre Koffmann, Raymond Blanc and Nico Ladenis. Later he was to become the youngest ever holder of three Michelin stars but before that, in 1987, he opened his own place, Harvey's, on Wandsworth Common:

Egon did more for British gastronomy than anyone else. He was a genius – his knowledge of food and wine was enormous. When I opened Harvey's Egon was the first critic through the door. I was Marco White but he was fascinated by my middle name. He wrote a review in The Sunday Times *in which he called me Marco Pierre White. I'm indebted to the great man.*

Thus Egon helped create the personal brand of one of our greatest chefs. In turn chefs such as Gordon Ramsay and Heston Blumenthal then learnt their craft working for White. By the 1980's Britain had woken up from its deep culinary slumber and it had discovered a restaurant culture. Egon wanted the rest of Europe to recognise this. He once helped organise a Euro-Chefs' competition in Spain via the International Academy of Gastronomes. He took John Burton-Race along to participate. He championed his cooking throughout and fought determinedly for Burton-Race to get a medal. And so he did – a gold medal, presented to the English chef by King Juan Carlos.

In November 1976 Egon decided to launch his 1977 Guide at Maxim's in Paris, for which he hatched an audacious plan. He took five British chefs who were being recognised in the Guide to cook a course each of an elaborate meal. These were they:

Terry Boyce, Carrier's, *Saffron soup with caviar*

Kenneth Bell, Thornbury Castle, *Mousseline of salmon*

Sonia Stevenson, Horn of Plenty, *Calves' sweetbreads with two sauces*

Murdo MacSween, Walton's, *Partridge with redcurrant stuffing*

Francis Coulson, Shannon Bay Hotel, *Syllabub*

It was, needless to say, all written up in *The Sunday Times* where Egon was described as "a small Hungarian with a hairstyle like a budgerigar". Great play was made of Egon's provocation: famous but stuffy old Maxim's had never had a woman cook in its kitchens before and refused to recognise that a dish called 'syllabub' existed. As ever, while getting all the publicity he intended for his Guide, Egon had some bigger statements to make too.

There was much, not always friendly, rivalry between the Egon

Ronay Guide and the older *The Good Food Guide*. The former was written by its team of inspectors, while the latter was mostly garnered from the contributions of its readers. Some preferred the literary style, the asceticism and the waspishness of *The Good Food Guide*. Others tolerated the flatter style of the Ronay Guide, valuing its reliability and sense of luxury. *The Good Food Guide*, edited first by Raymond Postgate and then Christopher Driver, was decidedly more idiosyncratic. The noted gastronome, Quentin Crewe, wrote in *Vogue* in 1975:

> *I used to favour* The Good Food Guide *but now would place infinitely more trust in Egon Ronay who, with the passing of the years, seems to have developed a far superior system of judgement to that of his rivals.*

Egon once challenged Driver as to why he had never included Inverlochy Castle in his guide (Grete Hobbs had attended a protest meeting of restaurateurs once where they had discussed how to counter what they saw as Driver's anti-capitalist, anti-luxury stance). Egon then went one step further and invited Driver to visit Inverlochy. Elizabeth Carter, who inspected for Egon and now edits *The Good Food Guide*, recalls that Driver gamely went but he stayed in the bed-and-breakfast at the gate, eschewing the comfort of the castle. He also arrived for dinner with his open-toed sandals and without a tie. They lent him one.

Another *Good Food Guide* Editor, Tom Jaine, felt that some of the Ronay entries were a bit bland but overall he is generous about Egon's legacy: "His views raised the standard of English cooking".

It was the keen competition between the two guides that led to my first meeting with Egon. I was producing a food show for BBC2 and

I had commissioned a number of reports from the then Editor of *The Good Food Guide*, Drew Smith. Egon was, I think, a little put out by this and pressed upon me the attractions of the Ronay Guide as a source of stories. He subsequently presented a number of very successful polemical pieces for me on such subjects as unpasteurised cheese, traditional apples and real game.

Over the years Egon shrewdly arranged for a long list of non-food companies and organisations to sponsor the Guides – Lucas, Dunlop, The British Tourist Authority, The Gas Council and Raleigh Bicycles are some examples. This enabled him to maintain and pay his team of inspectors. They were kept on a tight leash though. Simon Hopkinson, one of Britain's best cooks and an inspector in the late 1970's, remembers the hire car – a small, pale blue Ford Fiesta from Brew's of South Kensington. Hopkinson's broke down outside the main entrance of The Gleneagles Hotel and had to be pushed out of sight by the two porters. The inspectors' alcohol allowance was 50 pence per meal, and they were definitely not allowed to aggregate unused 50p's for a Friday blow-out of £2.50. But Egon treated his small team of inspectors as part of the Ronay family. At one time Hopkinson had two outstanding speeding charges on top of a previous conviction. Three endorsements meant suspension of his driving licence which he feared would lead to losing his job, being unable to travel. Egon paid for a barrister and got him off both charges. They remained good friends. Egon once again championed Hopkinson when he returned to cooking (though that did not deter Egon sending his celeriac soup back in Bibendum one day, complaining it was far too hot).

The schedules of the inspectors were worked out with care and precision. In September 1965 Egon hired an Australian divorcee to do this for him. She then moved on to designing the guide. Now also divorced, Egon married Barbara Ashton in 1967 and he then formally adopted her son, Gerard (assisting with his schooling and later enabling him to become a chocolatier). The Ronay Guides business was expanding rapidly at this point. Year after year his books appeared in the bestseller lists. In 1965 *The Financial Times* reported that the Ronay empire employed 50 people and had a turnover of £250,000 (more than £3.5 million in today's money). So Egon was now running a medium-sized publishing company and was able to announce in a trade magazine that he'd be doubling his advertising rates in 1966. He was producing a range of guides – to restaurants and hotels, pubs, ski resorts, one on Scandinavia and a brilliantly opportunistic effort in 1967 called *The Guide to Currency Holidays*. Harold Wilson's government had been panicked into placing tight restrictions on how much currency Britons could take on holiday with them, so this was a guide to cheap resorts and cut-price travel.

In 1974 he went further with his *In Britain* guide aimed at tourists in the UK. It included a survey of Soho clubs which noted that, "the days of the G string are over and nothing is left to the imagination". History does not record whom he sent as an inspector. In the early 1980's there were guides to the major cities of the world for the well-heeled and guides to transport cafes for the poor and parsimonious. Egon's guides were given widespread coverage in North America, with *The Washington Post* calling him, "the best known Hungarian in England". 'Egon Ronay' had become a well-known brand – a household name. Perhaps the best proof of this came in 1972 when the burlesque star, Fiona Richmond, was about to star in the soft-porn farce *Pyjama Tops*. It was well known that she had had hundreds of lovers around the world and that she had kept a careful record, rating all their performances. The tabloids dubbed her "the Egon Ronay of the bedroom". It was the value in this business and brand which Egon sold to the AA in 1985 when he was 70 – though he later had to sue to recover his name when it had been sold on and was being misused (see Dante Campailla's chapter).

On July 24th, 1995 a group of fourteen diners gathered in the private room of Les Saveurs in Curzon Street. Our host was Egon Ronay and he had prepared an exceptional dinner with the gifted French chef Joel Antunes:

Cream of celeriac with caviar
Taittinger Comtes de Champagne 1986

———

Sautéed fresh foie gras served with rhubarb
Krug Grand Cuvée

———

Chilled tomato consommé

———

Parmentier of lobster flavoured with truffle oil
Corton Charlemagne 1979 Bonneau du Martray

———

Roast smoked breast of duck in verjus sauce
Château Gruaud Larose 1983 St Julien

———

Feuillette of roast peach with verbena ice cream
Johannisberg Riesling 1983 Late Harvest (Napa Valley, Joseph Phelps)

———

Coffee and petits fours

What was the occasion? It was, of course, his 80th birthday. But Egon made no mention of that on the invitation or during the evening. It was clearly understood that we could eat, drink and enjoy spirited conversations but on no account were we to acknowledge the reason we were there. Why was Egon so secretive about his age as he got older? It was because he still had so many schemes and ambitions and, rightly, he believed that potential partners would think twice about such an elderly collaborator. He got away with it because of his vigour and because he presented much younger. For example, in 2000, when he was 85, the trade magazine, *Caterer and Hotelkeeper*, published a feature about him taking him at face value when he told them he was 72. But in 2005 the cat got out of the bag. Egon hosted a British Academy of Gastronomes dinner at The Dorchester where he was announcing the Grand Prix Award to the Prince of Wales for championing the revival of mutton. Hugo Rifkind of *The Times* was invited and wrote up the occasion for his newspaper's diary, noting that Egon was, in fact, 90. Egon felt that this damaged the various schemes that he was still busy plotting.

Grete Hobbs, the former owner of the Inverlochy Castle, asks with some force why Egon never received any recognition for his 50 years of food campaigns and his tireless proselytising on behalf of British chefs. In his tribute in this book Dwin Bramall calls it a travesty that Egon never received an honour. When he died *The Independent* made the mistake of saying he had never been offered one. The story is more complex than that. In 1994 I was walking over the Rialto Bridge in Venice with him on our way to an inkfish risotto dinner (see Nick Ross). He revealed to me that he had received a letter offering him an OBE but he was thinking of refusing it. What did I think? I thought that OBE was a very mean-spirited offer and that his achievements merited much greater recognition. Had he been a leading actor or a civil servant he would have been offered a more exalted decoration and yet would have affected our lives far less. But I was not surprised, it just demonstrated how some Britons still regarded food as relatively unimportant. I bit my tongue and asked him why he was minded to turn down the offer. He had a simple answer – someone whom he regarded as having done him a great wrong had been given the OBE the year before. He was not a vain man, but he was intensely proud. He could not stomach being categorised with a person he saw as his enemy. I agreed with him that the best course was politely to decline.

On subsequent occasions a number of us tried to get Egon at least a CBE. We packed the nominators with MP's, Lords and well known media folk but all to no avail. In the peculiar world of honours once you have declined one you will never be offered another lest it be thought you are negotiating for more elevated preferment. Shortly after Egon died I happened to be talking to someone on the Honours Committee which considered our final attempt. He said Egon was just too old. Too old be damned – PG Wodehouse received his knighthood in his nineties.

However, Egon did receive a higher and much more singular honour. On February 19th, 1977 he appeared on *Desert Island Discs*. Among his eight choices were Bela Bartok's 'Evening in Transylvania' and the Hungarian Radio and Television Symphony Orchestra playing variations on a Hungarian folksong. He told Roy Plomley that the folksong was his favourite piece. Was he a Hungarian Brit or a British Hungarian? Despite his 63 years in the UK he was and remained decidedly the latter. And we were very lucky to have him.

A Lionheart with a Steel-Trap Mind

Michael Edwards

People often ask me what it was like to work for Egon Ronay. Where to begin, with someone who was such an important part of my life for 40 years and the impetus behind my becoming a writer? First, abiding memories. Along with his great friend, the late Johnny Apple of *The New York Times*, Egon was one of the two most remarkable personalities in the quirky world of gastronomy I have ever known. He was a man of extraordinary drive and iron will: the embodiment of the Hungarian émigré, a force of nature who would follow someone into a revolving door but come out first.

His early life as the only child of Budapest's most successful restaurateur in the 1930's is well documented elsewhere in this book. But to get the measure of the young Egon two little insights are worth another airing. Both would stand him in good stead to become our most fearless food critic and a household name. Egon took a degree in law at Budapest University and might have gone on to postgraduate studies at Trinity Hall, Cambridge. But many things intervened, as Peter Bazalgette explains. Such a forensic mind was to know no fear when confronted by the threat of litigation over a coruscating column he had penned about some atrocity in British airport catering in the 1980s. Egon also had chutzpah in spades: when the Red Army laid siege to Budapest in 1945 and he put his famous blackboard outside his café saying 'business as usual', or when his family was rounded up by the Soviets as class enemies and Egon managed to pass himself off to his Russian guard as a 'waiter', both episodes Nick Ross describes in his chapter.

I first met Egon in 1971, having answered his usual small ad in *The Times* seeking applications for recruits to his expanding hotel and restaurant guide. It was a publication building a solid reputation as a user-friendly but seriously accurate alternative to the idiosyncratic *Good Food Guide*. Egon's increasing activity was well timed, as he had got wind that the first *Red Michelin Guide* to Great Britain was being planned. When it appeared text-less in 1974 it may have been a bible for the more traditional chefs, but it was to lag behind the ER Guide in putting bums on seats. Egon's methods of recruitment were typically shrewd and sophisticated. He often (though not invariably) preferred to have a team of well-educated people, generalists with a love and appreciation of classic cooking; crucially he looked for innate good taste, enough to recognise the exceptional on the plate and the finer aesthetics of the surroundings. Those of us who gingerly passed the test were mostly dilettantes, for sure, but probably better communicators and judges of the big picture than the majority of resting chefs and hotel managers also sometimes enrolled. These professionals were not always at ease with the written word. There were, of course, some wonderful exceptions, like Simon Hopkinson, the Lancashire chef who went on to make the reputation of Conran's Bibendum, in the old Michelin Building on the Fulham Road, and afterwards in a new career as a brilliant food writer, columnist for *The Independent* and television cook.

That first interview with the great man went smoothly enough. He smiled wryly when he read that I had spent a year in Italy before reading desultorily for the Bar, eventually abandoning the law for the wine trade. My main impression was of a dapper, immensely courteous man, with a steel-trap mind; he had hung his beautifully cut jacket on its Anderson & Sheppard hanger, donning a mohair cardigan at his working desk. He sent me off to have a trial dinner at some fashionable, rather good restaurant in a Knightsbridge arcade; it had a Sloane-ish ring to it, which now escapes me – Finola's maybe, the name of my first love, as it happens.

I wrote my positive report rapidly – it came very easily. About a week later, I heard that I was to be taken on for a month's trial period in Ireland with Major Donald Gray MC, Egon's general factotum, and a very clued-up young chef called Richard Page, one's of ER's soundest inspectors. Apparently my file said ". . . good taste, has journalistic bent". To be honest, I think I was being given an easier ride than I really deserved: a few days into the Republic, Donald took me on one side and said in a conspiratorial whisper, "I think you are going to make the grade". For the worst of reasons, it turned out – we had been to the same school! But it had one positive effect – having being locked up in one of those boarding schools with dismal food for five years, both

Donald and I independently determined to eat well for the rest of our lives. The Major could appear to be a rather starchy figure, with his eye patch and one good eye. But shyness hid a warm heart; he was an excellent cook and a fine judge of wine, as well as being an effective low-key advertising salesman. He was also a great schmoozer of industrial sponsors like Lucas and Dunlop, over a lingering lunch that was very '1970's'.

The month in Ireland was an Arcadian delight, particularly in Connemara on the west coast, eating oysters and wild salmon from the least polluted waters of Europe. Once, when we arrived in Galway, our cover was blown. Every hotelier and cafe owner on the west coast seemed to know we were around – the Gaelic bush telegraph transmitted gossip with astonishing speed. In Dublin, I ate one of the first truly grand dinners of my life at the restaurant of the Russell Hotel (now an apartment block) on St Stephen's Green. There, ordering eggs Benedict, I learned what Hollandaise sauce should really taste like. And I stared incredulously at the wine list, with Château Latour 1945 at £5, yes five pounds, a bottle. We drank well but never got to meet the mighty Pauillac, at least not on that occasion.

Back in London, on Planet Earth, I was given a hired Mini 850 in which I was expected to drive solo to any restaurant on the British mainland from Sutherland to Cornwall – Egon was always a master of limited resources! Each of the teams was given a ten-day schedule of places to visit, longer if one was far away. It was a solitary life: getting into a conversation at the bar was difficult for the obvious reason of preserving anonymity. I was often not thought to be an inspector as I usually ordered wine which was too good, mostly at my own expense – our wine allowance was one glass only of the *vin de la maison*. Egon, despite having a very fine cellar and being a munificent host, was himself abstemious and had a puritanical disapproval of his employees having a good time – on duty – with a half bottle of some jolly little Burgundy. But I look back with great affection on that carefree time before I got married. Comic situations were legion – like arriving marginally late in foggy November at Sheriff's House, a fine restaurant in Brockdish, Norfolk. There, hopping up and down in the car park, was the manically obsessive proprietor, Squadron Leader Pichel-Juan, mouthing the retort, "How can you expect to eat quenelles when you are four minutes late!" On a more basic level, Egon taught us to focus on what the researched restaurants set out to do, and how well they achieved it. In assessing the kitchen, we would choose dishes that tested the chefs' skills, always in line with the ambitions of the restaurant. In the relatively unsophisticated Britain of the 1970's, the staple tests were the house pâté, roast duck and crème caramel; little things like bread and coffee were as important then as they are now. But 40 years on, the emphasis has shifted more towards the quality of key delicacies, a thoroughly good development, with painstakingly made risottos served with fresh *ceps* or truffles, the signature *de nos jours*. I am not so sure about the preoccupation with gossamer-light textures in the cappuccinos and foams of molecular cuisine – as Patrick Michelon, the Alsatian maestro at the stove of the splendid Les Berceaux in Épernay puts it, "Texture is the issue, but not in the way the modernists think. Most *bons vivants* like to get their teeth into something." I'm pretty sure that Egon, looking down, would agree vigorously. Like most Hungarians, he loved game and would prepare it with the greatest care for his guests at Yattendon.

Perhaps even more important than the gastronomic guidebooks, in terms of his legacy, were Egon's tireless campaigns to improve the quality of British mass catering on the motorways, in hospitals, and later at the airports. When he arrived penniless at Victoria station in 1946, we all heard how Egon was affronted by the sight of that communal teaspoon dangling by a string from the ceiling at the station buffet, and he determined one day to do something about it. During the late 1970's and early 1980's, when he was the biggest name in food criticism and a familiar face in every living room, Egon launched a ferocious attack on the dreadful standard of staple foods and beverages in motorway service areas. He often crossed swords with Charles, Lord Forte. These encounters were the meetings of Greek with Greek. Both were small, pugnacious men of strong will; hardly an unbiased onlooker, I liked to think that Egon had the edge for his incisive intellect and even more for his boundless courage. He was truly a little lionheart, pitched against the juggernaut of Trust House Forte. One of the happiest and most positive projects in which I participated was ER's survey of food in the armed forces, also in the early 1980's. The quality of the soldiers', sailors' and airmen's meals was regularly irreproachable. I remember one lone moment of fame on the BBC Six PM Television News, singing the praises of exemplary fish 'n' chips on the deck of the aircraft carrier *Ark Royal*. Egon, inspired publicist that he was, played it for all it was worth.

In the mid 1980's, Egon made the one bad decision of his career. Finding it difficult to find continued sponsorship, he sold the rights of the guides to the Automobile Association for a very modest sum. "The worst thing I ever did," he later admitted. It was not until 2004 that ER got the rights back after lengthy litigation. In the meantime, among other consultancies, his organisation worked with the Wetherspoon pub group. I could never really understand why he accepted this commission: to put it kindly, all the food served in the group was *sous-vide* – very little was fresh food. It went against everything that Egon stood for.

Happily, he did have an Indian summer with his *Egon Ronay's 100 Best Restaurants*, published in 2005 and sponsored by the RAC. I was proud to take time off from wine journalism to work on this guide. Championing the rise of the Hibiscus restaurant, then in Ludlow, now in London, was a particular joy. I still believe that chef-patron Claude Bosi is one of the greatest exponents of modern cuisine working in Britain – because he can give his imagination full sway, based on the rock of a faultless technique learned in *stages* at most of the finest restaurants in France. Egon typically gave us full support and made Hibiscus Restaurant of the Year.

Like many great men, Egon was a mercurial character. If he had no respect for someone, he could be brutal and dismissive. Even as members of his coterie, we could all feel the sharp elbows of this human dynamo. But one could never be cross with Egon for long. He had the uncanny knack of dissolving all dissent and unhappiness in his circle with a wit and humour that was very endearing. My favourite memory of him was at the rehearsal for one of the launch dinners of the Guides at the Inn on the Park. When the banqueting manager addressed him as Mr Ronay, ER said "call me Egon . . . or better still Sir Egon – nobody else does!" He never did get that much deserved knighthood. Basically, I think it was due to his combativeness that he was never offered more than an OBE. He was a 'natural duellist', in Peter Bazalgette's perfect phrase, and probably made too many enemies. But Tuesday wouldn't have been Tuesday without having someone to row with.

Two close colleagues at Egon's have sent me their memories of the playfulness of the man and his great generosity. Roger Seal, my old friend now living overseas, agonized over his letter of application and stressed his lofty first ambition as a would-be barrister. He next admitted to an over-indulgent childhood, when going to the great tables of La Pyramide in Vienne and the Hotel de la Poste in Sens was something of an annual event with his parents. Roger then also cheekily suggested that the only thing that he could do to establish his *bona fides* as a thoroughly decent, God-fearing human being was for ER to contact his local vicar who would no doubt attest to his suitability for the job. Egon thanked Roger for his letter, saying that it at least showed a sense of humour. Could Roger phone his secretary and make an appointment to come in for an interview the following week? Roger went on to be one of Egon's most gifted inspectors and a good friend of the great man in later years. I think both characters recognised in each other the best sort of chutzpah that makes you smile. I know that Roger was wearing a white, black and red striped shirt (probably from Turnbull & Asser) identical to Egon's at their first meeting.

Michel Vigouroux, a colleague from the 1970's, also got in touch in France recently, renewing our friendship after a 40-year gap. He tells a charming story of how he told Egon he was going to Paris for the weekend, as he occasionally did. ER offered Michel dinner at La Tour d'Argent, with the advice, "Please yourself, go with someone and enjoy it. Don't look at the prices, choose whatever you want, and bring me the bill back." Magically, Michel found he was given the best table, overlooking Notre Dame. On another occasion, he went to Egon, saying he wanted to resign for a new venture in South Africa. After talking to him, as a father to a son, Egon asked whether getting an increase in salary would persuade Michel to stay. "My answer was 'Yes' and so I did stay on and never regretted it," says Michel. "I always felt respected and trusted; how could you not be loyal to such a character who has faith in you." Amen to that.

I also remember Egon for endless little kindnesses and for nudging me to become a Champagne scribe. Like Johnny Apple, another motivator of better writing, such men were larger than life and generous mentors. They are sorely missed.

The Lawyer's Lawyer

DANTE CAMPAILLA

I first met Egon Ronay as a guest of my old friend the late Sir John Plumb, then Master of Christ's College, Cambridge, at a London dinner of the British Academy of Gastronomes in the Marie Antoinette room of the Ritz Hotel in 1984. Plumb, who was President of the Cambridge Wine and Food Society, had told Egon of my enthusiasm for cooking and appreciation of good food. So when I was invited to join the Academy I readily accepted.

I soon discovered that in parallel with running his renowned Hotel and Restaurant Guides Egon had also founded the International Academy of Gastronomes in France. Then came the British Gastronomic Academy, with the aim of improving the standard of food and beverages at all levels of consumption in the UK. That company was dissolved in 1983 and Egon founded a new company called The British Academy of Gastronomes with the same aim (once satirically renamed The

British Academy of Gastric Gnomes by Loyd Grossman). Egon had no difficulty, with his great influence and reputation in the culinary world, in recruiting interesting members from a wide spectrum. Perhaps as a result of his charmed life in the cafe society of pre-war Budapest, he was particularly attracted to people with a title and distinguished careers and those who would now be known as 'celebrities'.

In 1984 the total membership of the Academy of 55 included, besides Sir John Plumb, Sir Alex Alexander (Chairman of J Lyons & Co), Johnny Apple Jr (London bureau chief of *The New York Times*), Jane Asher, Lord Briggs, Robert Carrier, Len Deighton, Charles Florman (European publisher of *Fortune* magazine), Sir Alexander Glen (past Chairman of the British Tourist Authority), the Earl of Gowrie, Allan Hall (author on food and wine), Rupert Hambro, Grete Hobbs (owner of Inverlochy Castle), Hugh Johnson, Prue Leith, the Earl of Lichfield, Ken Lo, Lord McAlpine, Sir Peter Parker, David Peppercorn, Patrick Rance (author on cheese), Albert Roux, Godfrey Smith, Serena Sutcliffe, Auberon Waugh, Jeffrey Wilkinson (MD of Lucas Industries), Charles Wintour (editor of *The Evening Standard*) to name but a few. I knew that Egon was hoping to bring in a High Court Judge, having studied law at Budapest University, but he settled for me as a common or garden solicitor on Plumb's recommendation.

We soon began to meet and phone each other frequently and our friendship gradually developed. I was intrigued by the contrasting facets of his complex personality. Although he had a wide range of acquaintances through his guides and Academy interests, it seemed he had made very few intimate friends since his 1946 escape to England from Soviet persecution in Hungary. Indeed, I believe he had never stayed the night with friends in a private house until he visited my wife, Jan, and me in Kent and later in our holiday home in Spain.

Whilst he epitomised *toujours la politesse*, he also thrived on confrontation. This was matched by his addiction to publicity, preferably by way of a combination of the two. It was a paradox that he particularly enjoyed press, radio and television exposure but invariably appeared as a measured and modest person. One thing was undeniable – he was a relentless workaholic with the most dogged tenacity.

Having sold his Guides to the Automobile Association in 1985 he was able to devote his energy and his distinctive palate (insured for a considerable sum and with the usual publicity) to his well understood mission to improve UK culinary standards across the board.

He was capable of flashes of *folie de grandeur* which I witnessed at first hand when he decided to expand the Academy. In November 1987 it had changed its name to the British Gastronomic Society. In January 1988, at the time when Rupert Hambro was the Chairman of the Society's Committee, he arranged for all members (thence to be called 'Fellows') to be notified that a circular letter was to be sent to 30,000 selected people with the aim of hugely increasing the Society's membership. However, this costly concept was frustrated by a libel action brought by Trust House Forte against the Committee members of the Society and Egon personally for criticism of that influential company's culinary standards. Egon had condemned the quality of their food at Heathrow in one of the Society's publications – one of the offerings was described as being "only fit for the dustbin". It was, of course, not the first time he had made such an attack – there had been smouldering disputes between Egon and Forte outlets for more than 20 years. This time Lord Forte reached for his revolver. Egon's solicitors, Kingsley Napley, vigorously defended the action with much enthusiastic support from Egon and the case was set down for hearing in May 1990. In the meantime the Society, whose assets had by then been considerably depleted, was to freeze its activities until the case had been heard. Rupert Hambro's name was removed from the Action following, to Egon's considerable dismay, his having expressed personal regrets to Rocco Forte. In the end the Fortes withdrew and paid substantial costs to Egon. The Society, nevertheless, had to be liquidated. The right to the use of the Academy name was retained.

This was a troubled period for Egon during which he was at great, personal financial risk but he remained undaunted. He was busily engaged in instigating the publication of *Great Dishes from the British Gastronomic Academy* under the consultant editorship of Allan Hall. He was also active in inspecting and improving food outlets at Heathrow Airport and publishing a widely circulated Airport Newsletter (ironically, following the imbroglio, BAA had contracted him to help them raise standards). This venture was followed by advising Welcome Break, one of the leading motorway caterers (see Richard Pennycook's chapter), and subsequently the high street pub group, Wetherspoon. Egon was never out of the media, attracting support and (occasionally hostile) criticism in equal measure. But he always gave as good as he got. This was exemplified in the following extract from a letter he wrote to *The Guardian* newspaper on August 18th, 2005, at the age of 90. Nothing escaped his eye and no ball bowled at him was ever left to go by :

Simon Goodley's Diary (17 August) suspected me of having changed my highly condemnatory views of one of the motorway caterers' (Welcome Break) food "once he started advising Welcome Break". In fact their then new Chief Executive had written asking me to help them improve their food and agreeing my criticism. This resulted in my company's huge, two-year operation (six full-time, professional inspectors, four administrative staff, daily two-page reports on outlets within every service station). In due course we did award stars for food though not in my Restaurant Guide but in passengers' leaflets to encourage the staff, such stars being awarded by Welcome Break with bonuses. The Diary also asks, tongue-in-cheek, whether my condemnation (15 August) of the oxymoronic name 'Gate Gourmet' of the catering company supplying airline food might amount to my 'touting for advisory work from airlines'. All my past three catering advisory activities (BAA, Welcome Break and the Wetherspoon pub group) resulted from the companies' approaches and – if I may add – were always successful.

From 1990 I acted as Egon's solicitor and was asked to incorporate a new 'British Academy of Gastronomes' with the same aim as his original Academy and membership limited to 60. Some of the original members joined the new Academy while others fell by the wayside, but the organisation flourished. Egon lost no time in ensuring that the activities of the new Academy, with his name in the forefront as President, kept as much in the public eye as the previous one. He was very proud of his PR skills and delighted at his 1990 coup of a half page in *The Sunday Times* covering the Academy's December dinner (with a fine photograph of Monsieur le President reading the menu). It was held at the Dorchester Hotel and reported on by Hugh Fearnley-

Whittingstall, no less. Further reports of the Academy's monthly dinners followed and their annual dinner to celebrate the award of the 'Grand Prix of Gastronomy' attracted wide attention. Egon then conceived the idea for subsequent Grand Prix dinners of inviting a troupe of distinguished chefs to execute the event, each being responsible for one course. This resulted in the 1991 Grand Prix dinner at the Inn on the Park (held through Egon's influence in association with Diners Club International) being created by Albert Roux, Anton Mosimann, Pierre Koffmann and John Burton-Race. *The Sunday Times* reported that the event was the culinary equivalent of Pavarotti, Domingo, Carreras and conductor Zubin Mehta appearing together on the same stage. News of the impending 1993 Grand Prix Dinner to be held at the Four Seasons Hotel took up a whole page in *The Evening Standard* with pictures of Egon and also Pru Leith as one of the invited guests.

Egon was always very active in supporting and encouraging promising chefs, who were invariably impressed with his taste for and knowledge of cuisine, in its widest sense. In 1995 he introduced an Egon Ronay Student Chef of the Year competition among selected UK catering colleges, and winners were invited, at the Academy's expense, to assist the master chefs at the Grand Prix annual dinners. Over the years the recipients of the Grand Prix awards included distinguished chefs, Jane Grigson, producers of Angus Beef, fine British Cheese, English mutton (in support of Prince Charles) and the food at the Tebay Services on the M6. With these awards Egon had found yet another way of promoting and rewarding excellence.

By 1994 new members of the Academy included Lord Ampthill, Peter Bazalgette, Field Marshal the Lord Bramall, Francois Brocard (London

Director of the Banque Nationale de Paris), Ronnie Corbett, Sir Peter and Lady Emery, Andrew Neil, Jeffrey Rose (Chairman of the RAC), Nick Ross and Sir Evelyn de Rothschild. Egon's reports to members of the Academy dinners were always acute and highly entertaining. After a dinner I had presented at Curzon Street's Les Saveurs restaurant in September 1994, his baroque comments on the main course were:

A bird, calling for straight treatment as grouse eminently does, always raises the hackles of a very French chef like Joel Antunes. So he took vengeance on the – in this case justified – British predilection for simple treatment, and ran wild. The grouse, instead of being roasted piano, was turned into symphony fortissimo: an exquisitely cooked breast of grouse, surprisingly well matched by truffled risotto and a daring but successful purée of damsons. The false note in the symphony came from a loud trombone of a sausage, perhaps Lyonnaise but rather Munichoisse, which I easily eliminated by pushing it to the rim of my plate. An exquisite, extraordinary, Euro-Scottish composition in which, true to form, the Germanic leitmotif sought prominence, this time in vain.

As a lawyer, acting for Egon was a considerable challenge. With his legal training he was an indefatigable drafter of his own agreements, about which I was often asked to comment only at the very last minute. He loved seeking my advice on innumerable matters and although he had the reputation of also obtaining second or even third opinions from acquaintances whose expertise he respected, we established a great mutual rapport.

Of course, before the war he had been offered a place at Trinity Hall,

Cambridge to read law, which he never accepted, deciding instead to go into the family hotel business. I still smile when I think of an occasion when we were both dining as the guests of Neil McKendrick, the then Master of Gonville and Caius, Cambridge. Egon, aged a very spritely 84, asked Sir John Lyons, the Master of Trinity Hall and a fellow guest, if the offer was still open, to which he, with a twinkle in his eye, replied, "Certainly for you, Mr. Ronay."

After the AA had sold his guides on to the Richbell Group, Egon was asked to participate in that Company's grandiose ideas for online expansion of guide activities. However, it gradually became apparent to him that the compilation of the guides was not being done according to his exacting standards. They still bore his name, of course, and this was jeopardising his reputation. Matters came to a climax in 1997 when my colleagues and I at Davenport Lyons were instructed by Egon to bring an action against the then owners of the guides (Egon took an immense interest in every step with a good degree of pleasure). This was an overwhelming success except that the defendants had no money to meet their liabilities. However, Egon achieved his principal aim – the right to publish the guides reverted to him. He had won his precious name back.

This event was widely reported and Egon was determined to undertake the uphill task of again producing an annual restaurant guide with the same degree of impartiality as of old, with independent and anonymous inspections by trained personnel and no payment or advertising by any of the listed establishments. He was sufficiently realistic to recognise the change in the economic climate since he had last published his guides. There was also the risk of increased competition from the plethora of restaurant reviews now in newspapers, magazines and online. In addition, it turned out to be much more difficult to obtain sponsorship and advertising from outside the food sector than in the past.

However, this was a challenge he could not resist and in 2005, at the age of 90, he succeeded in publishing, with the sponsorship of the RAC, *Egon Ronay's RAC Guide 2005 to the Top 200 Restaurants in the UK*. Unfortunately, in spite of vigorous promotion, the sales were disappointing, as was the demand for advertising. The digital era had arrived and all manner of free information was now searchable at the click of a mouse. However, Egon was sufficiently undaunted to bring out another guide in the following year. He even came up with a new angle – what he described as "A Heart Warming and very British Success Story: The Gastropub phenomenon". The result was *Egon Ronay's 2006 Guide to the Best Restaurants and Gastropubs in the UK*. In his foreword he wrote:

> *The word 'gastropub' itself is not an ideal one, in contrast to the products of the establishment to which it is applied, and one would be tempted to replace it with 'British bistro' were it not for the fact that the gastropub is such a thoroughly British institution.*

He also warned against raising prices to the level of restaurants and expanding dining rooms at the expense of bar space, thereby losing the essential pub character. Sales of this Guide were also disappointing in spite of widespread publicity, particularly in *The Daily Telegraph*. At this point Egon decided upon yet another approach to further his still-healthy business ambitions. Perhaps this was another example of *folie*, but you can't fault the energy of this, by then, 91-year-old.

For a number of years he had had his own website. But after the launching of his 2006 Guide he envisaged the creation of the (somewhat wordy) "Egon Ronay On-line, the sensationally new and by far the most extensive tasting-based food assessing operation in existence". To this end he prepared a detailed 20-page business plan for an entirely new survey of 200 motorway service areas, a weekly online restaurant guide, a newsletter, a banqueting and private rooms directory, not forgetting a hotel booking service. The plan also referred, for good measure, to future proposals for guides of chosen towns in the US and Europe, an "Egon Ronay Good Living Club" and a catering chain of coffee bars. He then set about contacting supermarket chains and other potential collaborators for sponsorship/investment to turn at least some of these dreams into reality.

His reputation was such that he invariably secured access to senior officials of the companies he approached. But unfortunately, although he was always given a courteous reception, all his attempts to attract interest in his schemes failed. I think he felt that once they met him they had reservations of partnering a man in his nineties. Perhaps unfair, but understandable.

Egon accepted the situation without rancour. Although I believe he understood his predicament, there was no question of his abandoning his search for new ventures. He still made stringent efforts to keep in the public eye, the elixir of his life. His blind tasting of supermarket Champagne at the Dorchester Hotel in 2006, assisted by Michael Edwards, one of his early guide inspectors, an authority on Champagne and a contributor to this book, earned considerable attention. And he never missed a suitable opportunity to write letters to the press on culinary topics which caught his eye, or indeed anything else (when the Romanian roots of the Conservative Leader, Michael Howard, were attributed to Transylvania, Egon claimed in *The Daily Telegraph* that most of that territory was really Hungarian, thus welcoming the Tory politician as a kinsman).

Egon had already taken the precaution of registering his name as a trademark, and following the frustration of his online hopes he next concentrated on seeking licensees for the use of his name to promote sales of commodities such as coffee, bread, sausages and soup. The condition was to be that his name would only be lent after exacting tastings and selection by him. As ever, quality control was everything and all would depend on his ultimate approval.

With tireless energy he spent most of his working days exchanging letters and e-mails, making phone calls and attending meetings (to which I was invariably asked to accompany him) with the wide range of companies he approached to achieve this aim. After each failure he would say to me, with a shrug of his shoulders, "Well, I'm not surprised – I would certainly never want to be in business with a man of my age". But he would already be devising a new proposal to put to another of his many food-related contacts.

His last business initiatives were then concentrated on appointing exclusive agents to market his name as a brand. However, when confronted with the standard form of agency licensing agreement, his habitual appetite for legal disputation got the better of him. Try as I might, I never succeeded in persuading him that the minutiae of these types of documents were not aimed at doubting his integrity or *bona fides*. Nor were they designed to curtail his right to object to any particular licensing of his name or the commodity to which it might to be linked. Although these agreements would indeed have given him prior approval to his heart's desire, we never seemed to emerge from the thicket of his objections. The result was that negotiations were both lengthy and never concluded.

For me, however, Egon remained a genuinely delightful companion. During our many enjoyable meals together and frequent telephone conversations, time never ever dragged. He loved to reminisce about his happy relationship with his highly successful parents. His grandfather had built the first of the family hotels (to be followed by other hotels and restaurants) in 1910. He was brought up as an only son enjoying a life of privilege. But this was firmly balanced with the discipline of the Piarist Fathers at the Jesuit College he was sent to. This inspired his passionate love of cathedrals, but he never gave any indication of having religious convictions.

He had an amazing knowledge of Hungarian history and liked to regale me with his detailed memories of those tumultuous times in Budapest prior to his escape to England in 1946. I tried for many years to persuade him to write his memoirs but sadly he died before he had written more than a short sample. The media has made much of his coyness about his age, but that was all about not wishing to prejudice future business rather than vanity.

He was often described as 'dapper'. Well, he was always very smart and had excellent taste in clothes, both formal and informal. It's fair to say that he had an old-fashioned antipathy for men dining in shirt sleeves or theatre-goers dressed as if for a picnic. As I hope I have demonstrated, he was not without an occasional quirk. He liked to convince me that an oyster could not be fresh if it did not wince to a squeeze of lemon.

I became a keen observer of Egon Ronay at the table. His invariable remedy for an occasional lack of appetite was an aperitif of brandy and soda. He loved strong black coffee (about which he was a true expert) "with a little cold milk on the side". For many years he had his own secret blend prepared by his favourite Mayfair supplier. He was a serious and perfectionist cook and in his last years still recalled the successful restaurant he had in Knightsbridge in the 1950's, expressing regret at not having one now. In later years he preferred his wife, Barbara, to prepare meals for guests. He adored her Irish Stew which – cooked on day one and eaten on day two – certainly merited his praise. Whilst particularly fond of French cuisine, he was an appreciative and constructive critic of the many ethnic cuisines. But he admired simplicity, disliking too many contrasting textures and flavours on the same plate. Although not wholly opposed he was sceptical about the latest fashion for Blumenthal-type, 'laboratory' cuisine.

He was very fond of the theatre and opera and a prodigious reader of biographies and history but not of novels, except for some Hungarian masterpieces. He adored Venice and at one time was seriously contemplating setting up a home there. He had an impressive knowledge of Venetian art and it was a pleasure to be guided by him around the Accademia. He was prone to occasional financial speculation but was not a regular gambler. However, at the Hennessy Gold Cup a few years ago, he placed his bets with great enthusiasm, having interrogated the bookmakers on the whole range of alternative bets, and was delighted at his beginner's luck.

How come he had such a long life? Many would doubtless like to believe a lot was due to his consumption of good food and wine, enjoyed without so much as a hint of gluttony. He ate with discrimination and care and never to excess. Egon certainly had little time for the modern paranoia about healthy eating. Although he was no hypochondriac, he liked medical consultations and would never hesitate to visit his trusted doctor even for a minor ailment (often subsequently inviting the specialists to Academy dinners). He expressed surprise about his long age but his philosophy was "carry on as best you can as if life were continuous".

I have no doubt that everyone who knew him will never forget him and that is what he would have liked most of all.

Inkfish Risotto and Fin de Siècle Brandy

NICK ROSS

I first got to know Egon on a rain-lashed water taxi one Friday night in Venice. I had heard that he and a few friends would nip abroad for a gourmet lunch, which seemed absurdly extravagant, but a weekend of fine dining in the city of canals was irresistible, and I quickly discovered why the trips were so unmissable.

Egon was a serious star. I had no culinary pedigree and as a newcomer to his little band of gourmets I was not sure what reception I would get from the master epicure himself. It turned out he was charming. In fact if there's one word that best defined Egon that was it. He was tiny, immaculately dressed and coiffured with a quaint, old-world politeness but the formality was quite without stuffiness. He welcomed me as though it was quite natural that I should accompany him on his latest gastronomic quest, as though my palate would be as sophisticated and my judgement would be as valuable as his. And that, of course, was his defining feature as a food critic. He wanted good food for ordinary people. Sure, he loved refined cuisine with the freshest ingredients and erudite service, but not every meal could or should be classy. It was even more important that day-to-day catering should be done well so that everybody had decent grub as a matter of course. Good food should be democratic.

It is a tribute to him that his democratic instincts should have survived so thoroughly from his early days in Budapest. His privileged upbringing as the son of the city's top restaurateur seemed destined to propel him into indulging the world's elite. Almost every day of his childhood he might be trying samples from the best chefs in Hungary or competing to see who could eat the most plum dumplings. He later described a charmed life as a young man in what seemed to him the carefree 1930's, racing from law studies to exotic parties and romantic balls or heady Christmas retreats to the snows above Kitzbühel. Fine food vied with wine and girls in their high life but he was never happier than pottering with friends in the kitchen or sampling the delights of cabbage soup, Gundel pancakes, May duckling or suckling pig* in his father's eateries or elsewhere in one of the city's many elegant garden restaurants.

History does not recall what mischief he got up to save one episode when he was 20 which says much about the period. It always haunted

---

*Suckling or sucking pig was a New Year's tradition in Budapest and Egon recalled how each December night an unfortunate piglet, squealing in terror, was hauled round diners, each of whom took a tiny snip of its downy hair for luck, before, held down by chefs, it was carried below. "The kitchen – resembling, with its herd of sucking pig carcasses and its frantic bustle, something between a veterinary morgue and a railway station – rose to the challenge of 750 simultaneous diners, focusing, by tradition, on the superb, crisp roast."

him and also József Zimányi, who writes about it elsewhere in this book. A well-heeled acquaintance insulted Egon and his best friend, apparently by making offensive remarks about a girl who was in their party while out on a social evening. At any rate it led to a challenge: there would be a pistol duel at dawn. Egon and his friend drew lots as to who should fight for the two of them and the friend drew the short straw. It must have been a sleepless night. Some time after 4 am Egon fetched the friend, their seconds and a doctor and set off with frayed nerves (not helped by the fact that he was a novice driver out without his parents' knowledge in his brand new car and on frozen roads). Egon skidded, collided with a lorry and had to sort out the accident while his compatriots found a taxi and headed off for the fateful rendezvous. When eventually Egon got underway again he passed an ambulance speeding from the woods and was panicked and appalled. He need not have worried. The ambulance was coincidence, the guns had been so cumbersome and the duellists so nervous that nothing hit its target, and everyone repaired to the Matthias Cellar restaurant for breakfast.

After university his apprenticeship took Egon into some of Europe's top establishments including the swanky Dorchester in London. But that gilded life was shattered by war, plunging him into a world of conscription and then deprivation. Egon had been brought up a Catholic (he played the organ at mass for four long years – which "put me off church for some time") but with his Jewish blood he must have felt uneasy in an army that sided with the Germans, even if the alternative was invasion from the east. When the Nazis occupied Hungary in 1944 the risk to his family became palpable. Egon himself avoided being labelled a Jew but neighbours informed on one of his uncles, who was rounded up and destined for the concentration camps. It fell to Egon to dig up an heirloom his family had buried in the garden, a gold cigarette box, and to try to bribe someone to get his uncle out. A German colonel obliged, drove with Egon through the winter landscape to the holding camp and demanded that the prisoner be placed in his custody. It worked. But the liberated uncle didn't seem to understand the risk his nephew had been taking. About half a mile from the camp he complained he was freezing and demanded they return to collect his wrap. Despite Egon's urgent protestations the colonel was determined to fulfil his bribed obligations to the letter. He turned the staff car round and this time demanded the prisoner's belongings.

The uncle survived the war in hiding and Egon survived without being denounced. But with his well-heeled background the Communists were almost as big a threat as the Nazis. When, by the summer of 1944, it was clear that the Reds were on their way to Budapest and ready to avenge themselves for Stalingrad, it was no longer an advantage to be the son of one of Hungary's top pre-war taxpayers, even if by the time the Russians stormed the city Egon was hungry and cowering in a cellar like everyone else.

Some 60 years later Egon went back to Budapest and showed us where retreating German tanks had ploughed through one of his father's largest restaurants. We heard at first hand a story I later came across in his self-published autobiography, *The Unforgettable Dishes of My Life*. There was a hiatus between the outgoing Nazis and the incoming Russians. The temperature was minus 20°C and, apart from a few people hacking frozen meat off dead horses, the streets were deserted, the shops closed and all was desolation. The vast Ronay restaurant was wrecked. There were no windows and there was no food.

But in one's twenties, life cannot stop. Two of our old head waiters appeared and we cleared a small corner of the restaurant, 'requisitioned' a tiny, wood fired stove from an empty flat, broke up a few restaurant chairs for fuel and started brewing ersatz coffee; the retreating Germans had taken everything else with them. I scrawled 'OPEN' on a piece of large cardboard and misspelt it in the excitement. Ill-clad cellar dwellers emerged, unbelieving.

Egon was thrilled to think that he had opened Budapest's first post-war cafe and soon after he was instrumental in fixing a memorial plaque there to commemorate the first premises of any kind to get going after the siege: "This plaque was erected by the free trades union of the workers in the catering industry, in memory of the opening of the Belvárosi Cafe under the management of Miklos Ronay and his son on the 18th February 1945, the first business to open after the siege of the capital."

As it happens, his enterprise also saved his life. From the start of the Russian occupation patrols began arresting people more or less at random to seek out bourgeois enemies of the state and Egon was hauled, "terrified to death", to a barracks to be vetted. Miraculously, the guard assigned to him was a soldier to whom he'd served coffee three days before. Egon desperately tried to remind him that he was a 'worker': "'Tovarish . . . I serve . . . waiter . . . work with my hands.' He remembered, broke into a smile and translated. I was free."

Egon's whole life was an adventure, and at first I suspected his anecdotes were so extraordinary that they must have been embellished, but they weren't. No sooner had he evaded deportation to Siberia than he was flabbergasted to be promoted by the new regime to organise the feeding of the highest-ranking Soviet officers (see Paul Fabry's chapter). The newly installed Hungarian President demanded state banquets and Egon was "overawed hovering in the dining room around guests who included Voroshilov, Gromyko, who was then a political adviser, and Stalin's son".

His escape from Communism, aided by a bribe and a lot of vodka, was another unlikely but true story, as was his arrival as a refugee in London in 1946 and his horror at his first taste of British railway station catering where, if he wanted sugar (and he was lucky to get it amid post-war austerity rationing) he would have to use a single dirty spoon dangling from the grubby string.

All in all it is little wonder that Egon was as passionate about public food wherever it was served, in transport cafes, pubs, airports or motorway diners, as he was about Michelin-starred establishments. And no doubt that was also why he thought the Michelin too pompous, too haughty, and too concerned with white starched linen rather than the simple perfection of the food.

It had been Fanny Cradock who tempted him to write about restaurants rather than manage them and I was struck by his recollection that in those days the chefs were unknown and considered unimportant. It was the maître d' who made or failed to make a place, and evidently Egon had been a successful one. His father had arranged good introductions for him in London and he managed several restaurants before borrowing a sizeable sum, starting a place of his own and introducing French cuisine to Knightsbridge. But of course it was once he'd started writing that Egon Ronay truly came into his own. He could be frank in his assessments but, like a gastronomic Simon Cowell, even his most acerbic judgements were simply honest, and usually right. His passion was not to criticise but to improve, and with his old-world charm he delighted in nothing more than discovering a new eatery with a budding genius in the kitchen.

Anyhow, I digress. We were in Venice on my first trip with him long after his Guides had made him famous and when, sadly, their success was a fading memory. But though now in his late seventies he was full of the joys of spring. The same could not be said of the Venetian weather. It was raining, dark and stormy. Egon had booked us all into one of Venice's finest (and most expensive) hotels, the Cipriani, which he adored and where the manager, Dr Natale Rusconi, was a hotel industry legend and, therefore, naturally an old friend. All visitors to the Cipriani feel special from the moment their water taxi pulls up to the jetty, but with Egon we were clearly VIP's. We were met with a flurry of umbrellas and escorted to our quarters, visiting each other's rooms with excited oo's and ah's. Naturally Egon and Barbara's suite had the finest view in town.

And so to my first dinner with Egon, setting off in the dark across the water under a crashing rainstorm and getting wet as we made an undignified sprint into the restaurant. It was fun, the wine flowed and then, as the first course was cleared away, Egon turned to me. What, he asked, did I think of my squid ink risotto? Actually it had been impeccable, genuinely memorable, and I was quietly relieved when he seemed satisfied with that hyperbole without demanding a thorough review – the more so when I later discovered that inkfish risotto was one of his great favourites.

Back at our hotel Dr Rusconi gravely approached us and asked whether we could assist him. Could we please accompany him to a nearby room? Bemused but wishing to oblige, we followed him to find a long table with a line of ancient Armagnac and brandy bottles arranged from one end to the other. "I'm having some difficulty," said Il Dottore. "I can't decide whether the 1889 is better than the 1893, the 1894 or the 1896. Or perhaps the 1923. Would you be so kind as to taste it and give me your view?" We duly obliged and after much consideration declared that the twentieth-century tipples were decidedly better than their forebears. I had also concluded by then that Egon was clearly a man to tag along with.

So it went on over the coming months and years with every place we ate. We dined a lot, and usually we ate extraordinarily well, looked after with special attention by managers and proprietors, waiters and sommeliers. Yet none of it was fawning on a food writer who had enormous influence, because by then his influence had waned. It was friendship and admiration for a man with prodigious talent and exquisite taste who shared their passion for food and wine.

His Guide had truly been the holy grail. More accessible, less stuffy, much more detailed and, in Britain, much more widely read, than any other, it set high standards for itself as well as for the institutions it appraised. The inspectors were anonymous and wholly independent, and no establishment could be included without at least one annual visit and sometimes several. It was a costly business in food bills alone. But it had purity, unlike the online guides of today, whose supposedly impartial reviews have proved to be manipulated by proprietors or others with an axe to grind.

In his eighties and even nineties he was always frustrated that the Guide was a thing of the past, always ringing up with a new idea for an online version or some other wheeze, and I suspect he was disappointed that his fame was fading and was fearful his legacy would be overlooked. (Even so, in the last year of his life when he came round to supper my young nephew was struck by the unusual name of the visitor we were expecting. "Egon," he said, "you mean Egon as in the name Egon Ronay." When he discovered it really was the diminutive white-haired gourmet he was "dead impressed".)

In Egon's final months his memory faded, much to his annoyance. The last time I dined with him he was embarrassed to have forgotten why the occasion was special (it was a rehearsal with my wife for a wedding anniversary lunch). Nonetheless, his ability to detect flavours was, as always, a marvel and his judgement was as sharp, and as blunt, as ever.

I think he would have been quietly thrilled that his death was greeted with such dismay and with so many glowing tributes. He need never have worried that his contribution to British life would be overlooked. He was the high priest of eating out. The measure of his influence is that London now has at least as many fine restaurants as Paris. We British, whose food was once a joke, are now as knowledgeable and keen on gastronomy as anyone. It is a splendid, and remarkable, legacy.

Egon, we all miss you.

Eating with Egon

Francois Brocard

During the 1990's and beyond, Egon Ronay and a small group of friends made occasional forays to sample the cuisine of Europe's finest chefs and cooks. I was one of the flying diners and here I have picked out a few of the exceptional menus – all a testament to Egon's appetite and staying power. How did he eat and drink so persistently in the world's best restaurants but live to 94? He was always moderate in his consumption, and took the precaution of exercising every morning of his life.

1994 FREDDY GIRARDET, CRISSIER IN SWITZERLAND. LUNCH

15th October. A day trip from London for an excellent three-star Swiss lunch. One of our first gastronomic excursions with Egon. The best sorbets of the year. What we didn't know at the time was that Egon had supplied FA Cup Final tickets for Girardet not long before. So it was always going to be a special lunch.

Homard Breton aux artichauts et gribiche safranée au jus de corail

Tortelloni de poule faisane aux truffles blanches

Étuvée de Saint-Jacques aux coquillages et à l'osciètre

Rouget de roche en filets poêlés à la tapenade, boulangère
d'herbes aux saveurs provençales

Canard nantais au vin de Pommard

Fromages frais et affinés

Dacquois d'ananas

Sorbets et glaces du jour

Friandises

———◆———

Champagne Blanc de Blancs Grand Cru, Selection F. Girardet

Vernaccia di San Gimigniano 1991, Teruzzi & Puthod

Vouvray sec 'Le Mont' 1992, G. Huet

Pommard 'Les Epenots' 1985, J Parent

Grain Noble 1991, M.-Th. Chappaz

rtichauts
us de corail

e faisane
nches

nt-Jacques
ges et à l'osciètre

ts poêlés à la tapenade,
ux saveurs provençales

s au vin de Pommard

ges frais et affinés

acquois d'ananas

bets et glaces du jour

Friandises

rissier, le 15 Octobre 1994

1995 YAN-KIT SO, AT HER HOUSE IN WEST LONDON. DINNER
25th February. A private dinner prepared by our friend and noted
Chinese food writer, Yan-kit So. Sumptuous pig's trotters with ginger –
a dish usually associated with the birth of a child.

Salade tiède with dried oysters and quail
Spicy wriggling tiger prawns

———◆———

Pig's trotters with ginger

———◆———

Steamed roast duck stuffed with glutinous rice
Monk's vegetables

Sat. 25 February · 1995 Year of the Pig

Yan-kit So
11 Gordon Place London W8 4JD
Tel. 01 937 1413

Salade tiède with dried oysters + quail
Spicy Wriggling Tiger prawns
Pig's trotters with ginger 豬腳薑先醋
Steamed roast duck stuffed with glutinous rice
Monk's Vegetables 羅漢齋

1996 L'Ambroisie, Place des Vosges, Paris. Lunch

15th June. Lunch for eight at the table of the three-star chef, Bernard Pacaud. Lobsters and Poulardes aux morilles! A photograph was taken of Egon puffing on a monster cigar afterwards. From the photo Barbara Ronay painted the splendid portrait that sits on the cover of this book. The precise wines are lost in the mists of time.

Navarins de homards Bretons, pommes de terre fondantes au romarin

Poulardes aux morilles

ou

Pigeons aux girolles

Sélection de fromages frais et affinés

Tarte fine sablée au chocolat, glace à la vanilla

ou

Soupe de fraises au coulis de mangue, meringue perlées

———◈———

Champagne Roederer

Chateauneuf du Pape

Château Figeac

Porto

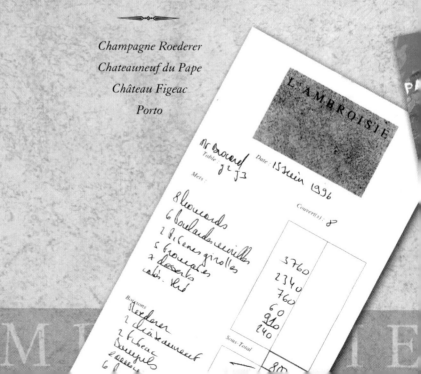

1997 PAUL BOCUSE, COLLONGES-SUR-SAONE, LYONS. LUNCH

7th September. The meeting of two great gastronomic men – Bocuse and Ronay. A perfect, classical menu with the truffle soup and the famous Canette de Bresse, carved in thin slices at the table. Bocuse much in evidence and characteristically anxious to sign our menus.

Amuse-gueule de l'Auberge
Soupe aux truffles noires V.G.E.
(dish created for Président Valéry Giscard d'Estaing 1975)
Gratin d'écrevisses Fernand Point
Loup en croûte à la mousse de hommard, sauce Choron
Granité des vignerons au Marc du Beaujolais
Canette de Bresse rôtie à la broche
Sélection de fromages frais et affinés 'Mère Richard'
Crème brûlee à la cassonade Sirio
Delices et gourmandises, petits fours et chocolats

❖

Magnum de Dom Pérignon 1988
Condrieu 'la Doriane' 1995, E Guigal
Côte Rôtie 'Brune et Blonde' 1993, E Guigal

1998 GORDON RAMSAY, CHELSEA, SOUTH-WEST LONDON. DINNER

Autumn at Gordon Ramsay's newly opened Royal Hospital Road restaurant. A moderate number of courses in a French-style menu, but cooked very much à la Gordon. Egon approved of British menus in English, whatever the cuisine.

Rillette de canard

Bouillon de poule with white truffle oil and julienne of vegetables

Roasted tranche of foie gras pressed with pheasant and served with pickled girolles

Panaché of sautéed sea scallops on a bed of cauliflower purée with beignets, white raisin vinaigrette

Pigeon from Bresse poached then grilled, served with a swede purée and truffle sauce

Rum and caramel panna cotta

Hot fondant of chocolate with vanilla ice cream

Coffee and chocolates

———◆———

Laurent Perrier, cuvée Grand siècle NV

Pouilly Fuisse vieilles vignes, Manciat-Poncet 1995

Chorey-les-Beaune, domaine Maillard 1995

Rivesaltes, Château de Canterrane 1976

'98.

canard

h white truffle oil and
of vegetables

e of foie gras pressed with
erved with pickled girolles

autéed sea scallops on a bed of
ower purée with beignets,
hite raisin vinaigrette

from Bresse poached then grilled,
with a swede purée and truffle sauce

Rum and caramel panna cotta

te with vanilla ice cream

1999 MARTIN BERASATEGUI, GIPUZKOA, NORTHERN SPAIN. LUNCH

18th July. A trip to Spanish Basque country to discover one of the best restaurants in Europe. Smoked eel, foie gras and green apple – a great starter – followed by, among nine others, a wonderful grilled pigeon served on pasta fresco with black olives. Note Egon's handwritten comment, top left of the original menu below: "This is a meal that gastronomic poems are made of."

Com el milhojas caramelizado de anguila ahumada, foie gras,
cebolleta y manzana verde

Ostria fría con crema de coliflor y jugo espumoso de remolacha

Toffe de mantequilla salada de guisantes con gelée de percebes

Cigala salteada con ravioli cremoso de cebolleta, puerros jóvenes
y vinagreta de yemas trufadas

Gelatina caliente de sopa de pescado con ensalada de frutos del mar

Mendresca asada con trigo cocinado y navajas salteadas

Pichon asado sobre pasta fresco de queso, verduras y aceite de olivias negras

El jugo ligero de naranja, compota de kumquat con fresas de gariguettes,
granizado de whisky y helado de cáscara de limón

El cacao frío con falso crep de yogur casero y sorbet de fruta de la pasión

———⊰⊱———

Gran Caus 1996 (Carles Esteve Grewwe) D.O. Penedes

Bodego Castano, Hecula 1995, D.O.Yecla

Pedro Ximines Vino Dulce del Poste , D.O. Montillo Morilles

This is a meal
that gastronomic
poems are made of
Egon Ronay

so much a meal as a work of art.
course a Renoir.

Inspired by the Brockards —
18/7/99

An entirely memorable lunch
with those of like-mind.....
at last gastronomy
(Martin Berasategui)
M.B.

MENÚ

Comenzará con estos aperitivos:
ENSALADA DE PIMIENTOS, ASADOS A LA LEÑA, CON ANCHOA MARINADA.
EL PASTEL DE QUESO DEL PAÍS, ASADO AL HORNO, CON JAMÓN.
TARTARE DE VERDEL Y RAPE.
SOPA.
CON EL MILHOJAS CARAMELIZADO DE ANGUILA AHUMADA, FOIE
CEBOLLETA Y MANZANA VERDE.
GRAN

2001 Nadia Santini at dal Pescatore, near Mantua. Dinner
10th November. A restaurant in the marshes where frogs' legs gratinées
and grilled eels are an essential part of the local feast, as well as saffron
risotto with fried artichokes and horse casserole with polenta (history
doesn't relate what we drank). Egon enjoyed the Saturday night dinner
so much he proposed we return for Sunday lunch. We did.

Terrina di Salmone, Astice, Olio extravergine e Caviale

Asetra Malossot

oppure

Culatello di Libello, Gras Pista e Polenta, Salame Moantovano

Risotto con Pistilli di Zafferano e Carciofi Fritti

Anguilla del Lago alla griglia, con insalata verde e cipollotto

oppure

Coscette di rane gratinate alle Erbe fini

Stracotto di Cavallo, verdure di stagione servitor con polenta

Formaggio

Dolci

An Inspector Calls

RICHARD PENNYCOOK

I n the patchwork quilt of my early childhood memories, Egon Ronay
occupies more than one square. His name symbolised, for many
years, something that was appealing, desirable but unattainable.

I was a child of Second World War parents who suffered the Blitz,
evacuation and rationing. The generation for whom whale meat was
necessary protein and bananas a rare treat. The generation that Egon
Ronay tried to educate, painstakingly, in the life-enhancing joys of
good food.

My earliest memories of the name Ronay came during family
holidays in places such as Newquay and Keswick. My parents, from
solidly working-class stock, aspired to be middle class. Dad, one of
seven children, was the first to gain a degree and earn a salary rather
than a wage. We owned a house, but money was always tight and, in
most things, we would make do and mend. So it was that our holidays

were self-catering, with one 'meal out' designed to be the high point. But how to choose? A wander through town, with window shopping of the menus displayed in tea-houses, pubs and restaurants, was the usual technique. We would end up at 'The Poldark Tavern' or 'The Wordsworth Cafe', and in later years – as our sophistication and disposable income grew – 'The Berni Inn'. Not, however, before passing one or two establishments sporting 'Egon Ronay Guide' plaques on the wall. When I pointed out the obvious attractions of these places, like white tablecloths and uniformed waiters, my sister and I would be hurried away, with an explanation that they were "not for the likes of us". Instead, we would feast on steaks that would surely pass no DNA test today, potatoes complete with eyes, and vegetables boiled to within an inch of their lives (just as my mother did at home).

So it was that I grew up with the name 'Ronay' lodged in my psyche, along with other unattainable, unscaleable heights – fast cars, exotic destinations and elegant women.

When I started working and earning a wage, I soon found that whilst looping a Ferrari through the Rascasse to play a hand of Chemin de Fer at the Casino remained a distant dream, dinner at an Egon Ronay rated restaurant was within savings-reach. Initially, three or four months' saving would be rewarded with an experience in the middle of the rating range. I discovered the joy of good food, and the Egon Ronay Guide held my hand the whole way. After a while I realised that purchasing five-year-old copies in the second-hand bookshop was a false economy. Instead, acquiring a trophy copy on publication day became as satisfying as a glass of Beaujalais Nouveau that had been trucked through the night in order to attain a headline. The Guide was brilliant

– it tracked year by year our journey to becoming a foodie nation, whilst also recording our cultural and geographic diversity and, inadvertently, setting some of today's 'celebrity chefs' on the path to over-exposure. I was fortunate, through Egon, to discover the likes of Michael Caines, Tom Aikens and Jean-Christophe Novelli at an early stage.

Roll forward 15 years and Egon himself clattered into my life for real. It was April 2000 and I had just been given a new job – Chief Executive of Welcome Break, the UK motorway services business. The company's financial performance was poor, and its reputation with customers worse. I knew the job would be trying, but I had not remotely contemplated being caught in the midst of an 'Egon event'. There it was, however – first day in the job and we were on the front page of *The Daily Mirror* and featured in all the other papers – "Egon Ronay slams motorway food". Egon, the consummate marketeer, was using a 'splash' headline about the culinary disaster discovered by his inspectors to achieve two things at once – focus on the continuing food desert that was the motorway service station (first highlighted by Egon in the 1960's) while simultaneously driving the sales of his latest guide – his habitually clever focus on the brand Egon Ronay.

I wrote to Egon that day, saying that I agreed with him absolutely and would like his help to fix the problem. Egon replied by return, but with caution. The challenge intrigued him, but he was naturally distrustful of a big corporation apparently seeking his endorsement. Once given, would it cost him his independence? One meeting followed another, and I believe Egon began to see that I was a genuine admirer, as concerned as he was not to see him compromised. So a deal was struck – Egon would have full 'editorial' control over all our food ingredients, and his inspectors would conduct a programme of unannounced inspections on our premises and grade them. When I naively suggested a rating scheme from one to three stars, Egon pointed out that nil would have to be the starting point.

The first step was to set up a test kitchen at one of our sites. I was fortunate to have the support of Nicky Ison, a food technologist who had worked with Egon before, and whom he trusted. Nicky set about testing the 600 food ingredients produced on our menus. Egon tasted every one, and rejected three quarters. It was a grisly task – our sausage skins were specified to a thickness that would allow deep-frying in batches of 200 and our coffee was frequently kept warm in an urn for four hours. Whatever Egon rejected, we changed. The sausages alone cost us an extraordinary quarter of a million pounds per annum to rectify. Some colleagues were sceptical, particularly when Egon insisted we chop capers and hand-make our tartare sauce, because none of the factory made alternatives were acceptable.

Alongside the refreshing of all our products, Egon began to train and educate our staff. His passion, bordering on missionary zeal, soon began to win converts. Managers were taken to Carluccio's, and given tutored tastings of the freshest and best ingredients. Catering assistants were treated to dinner at The Savoy. Eyes were opened.

The next, biggest stage of the process was for Egon and a small, trusted team of inspectors to arrive unannounced at our sites and test the food. Detailed reports followed, and at first they were head-in-hands lamentable. Gradually, people began to rise to the challenge – competitive pressure was a powerful motive force. After a number of weeks, the first 'one star' report arrived, and was duly celebrated. Before long, a 'three star' award was given, and we felt confident enough for me to appear on BBC Radio 2's Jimmy Young show (at the time the largest radio audience in the UK) to claim that with Egon's help we were transforming motorway food. With Egon's exacting standards and absolute integrity, it was simply the case that any customer eating in a 'starred' restaurant was experiencing better food than ever before in the history of motorway services. Inevitably, our competitors began to take note and to respond, so that over a period the industry pulled itself up by its bootstraps.

Working with Egon was a delight. His dedication to the task was enormous, and he regularly left people half his age panting in his wake. Whether dealing with a chairman or catering assistant, he was unfailingly polite, and a terrific sport. He attended a raucous awards dinner to hand out prizes to successful teams and toured our sites the length and breadth of the motorways. Humouring *The Caterer and Hotelkeeper* magazine, who wanted an article, he allowed an over-fussy photographer to keep him standing for an age on a wind-blown motorway bridge in freezing temperatures. Only when dealing with fools or frauds did Egon ever become difficult.

Through working together, Egon and I became friends, and in due course the friendship extended to his wife, Barbara, and to mine, Sue. Always, the common thread was food, initially as his guest at the Academy of Gastronomes, and then on through the best kitchens in the land. One of my greatest pleasures and, I hope, his, were long lunches at The Savoy, Claridges, Tom Aikens, Gordon Ramsay, et al whilst discussing the state of the world. Egon's personal history was fascinating (as other contributors to this book demonstrate), and he was widely read. He had sharp insights into most things, and clear opinions on many people. On these occasions, we took it in turn to book, and I soon realised that when the table was in my name Egon's arrival unannounced could cause great commotion. The high esteem in which he was held, throughout the restaurant world, survived long after his retirement.

My last long lunch with Egon was at The Connaught, after his illness had begun to take hold. For me, it was a poignant occasion, as the realisation dawned that a relationship which really did feel as though it had lasted a lifetime was now coming to an end. For all of us, whenever we encounter good food in this country – in restaurants, pubs, airports or motorway service stations – we should remember that Egon led the revolution.

Le Stilton Anglais

Godfrey Smith

One morning 11 years ago I met Egon as planned at Heathrow. It was a rendezvous worthy of Le Carre. Egon looked at his most conspiratorial – a mode well suited to his Hungarian ancestry. He carried a large carrier bag – or rather two such bags – the better to disguise the contents."It smells to high heaven," he confided. "I only hope they let us through customs."

The bag, or bags, contained, it emerged, a prime English Stilton, bought that morning at Neal's Yard. Egon was taking it to Paris as a present for the Academie des Gastronomes – that coterie of 40 French foodies who lead the entire nation in reverent worship at the shrine of the greatest cuisine in the world. They always used to meet at the same restaurant – Maxim's – and eat a lunch or dinner previously devised by one member. It's reverently cooked and eaten, first at a dress rehearsal so that any imperfections can be identified and eliminated. There are only four honorary members and Egon was one of them. He had been asked by his confreres to present another lunch; it was, they said, too long since his last.

On that previous occasion, Egon confided to me, he had dropped a clanger. Anxious to show the flag for English cooking, he'd presented the Academie with Beef Wellington – only realising too late the unfortunate resonance of that word in French ears. So the Stilton was by way of a peace offering, majestic pong and all. Happily, the customs let it through and we carried it safely with us to the lunch at Maxim's.

I'd always assumed that the French Academie would be peopled entirely by ancient, bearded old Frogs who looked like the brothers Goncourt or the great Sainte-Beuve himself. Not a bit of it; they turned out to be a tableful of well-groomed, gossipy, fortyish businessmen who all spoke impeccable English. Egon presented his lunch in what he said was his kitchen French; it sounded pretty stylish to my untutored ears. He had meant to give them Poulet de l'Empereur, but the particular truffles needed to give it that divine flavour were not available in Paris just then so he'd settled for the classic French dish Coq au Vin instead.

This went down well with the academicians, who told me that – *hélas* – nowadays it was rare even in bourgeois France to find it properly done. We started Egon's lunch with a simple whiting, and ate, for our positively homely pud, cherries in syrup with vanilla ice cream. But the pièce de résistance that day was unquestionably Le Stilton anglais. It drew loud plaudits even from those extremely learned Frenchmen. Egon's previous faux pas over the Beef Wellington was forgiven and forgotten.

Egon was not the first to give us an annual guide to the places where we could find the best cooking in our draughty little island. That honour must go to Raymond Postgate (1896-1971), socialist historian, detective novelist and classical scholar, who published his first *Good Food Guide* in 1951. It was written by amateurs for amateurs; that was its charm. Egon was a professional. He too started modestly. He published his first restaurant guide eight years later, in February 1959. It was a little pink book priced at three shillings. In his early years he was maligned because his English was not then as urbane as it might have been and certainly dim little words like 'tasty' and 'cosy' surfaced too often.

It was a curmudgeonly charge to bring against a man who had arrived here in 1946 with limited English. The infelicities were ironed out, and he went on to fight the good fight for 40 more years after Raymond had gone. He accepted sponsorship, but it was always in the public domain, not a covert influence, and it enabled him to pay inspectors. He won some famous battles in his 94 years against the horrors that lurked in our kitchens. No one more than Egon enjoyed a right dust-up with philistine restaurant chains or unhinged celebrity chefs; but his war is not over yet and probably never will be.

"There is still a smirk on the newscaster's face when the subject of good eating comes up," he used to chide. "The sauce bottles that were fixtures on a past British prime minister's table are still regarded as endearing signs of his British homeliness, whereas they would have lost millions of votes for President Mitterand." It's no secret that Egon turned down the OBE he was offered, not because it was a slight on him but because it was an insult to the miraculous change for the better that cooking had enjoyed here under his benevolent aegis. He should have been Sir Egon years ago.

He was a tiny, dapper, charming little chap with exquisite manners and a delicious sense of humour. He liked to relate how he had popped the question to his future wife, Barbara, over a lovingly chosen dinner and some gluggable wine in a romantic Chelsea restaurant. She was touched – yet dismayed. "But Egon," she protested. "I can't cook." She was being much too modest. Her Irish Stew was and is a stupendous dish. In any event Egon did not believe in haute cuisine at his own table. If you were invited to dinner there, you could be sure of very good raw materials and some delicious wines – but everything he offered was simple and unpretentious. Similarly, he was an appreciative guest if he came to your own house. We once gave a Sunday lunch in the country for our neighbour Jane Grigson. Egon and Barbara were there and enjoyed the roast beef and apple tart as much as anybody.

He retained all his life the seductive old-world style of his native Budapest. And woe betide anyone who broke its unwritten rules. When some benighted young PR girl he'd never heard of came on the phone one day and greeted him with "Hello Egon", he replied politely, "Please forgive me, but I forget – where it was that we were introduced." He found England a culinary wasteland and left it a place where meals were beginning to be no longer a pit stop or a penance but occasions for dalliance and delight. It was a privilege to have known him – and what a pleasure.

The Man Who Taught Britain How to Eat

MICHAEL WINNER

Food critics are the most useless people in the world. None of them knows what they're talking about. They're pompous, arrogant show-offs who write in overflowing sentences about sauces that no one knows or cares about. There was only one exception and he died last year, aged 94, at his home in Berkshire. His name was Egon Ronay.

He was a quiet, dignified man, whose father had five restaurants in Budapest. The business was destroyed when the Russians took over during the Second World War. Egon was reduced to selling coffee from a stall. Then he was imprisoned in a basement to be sent to Siberia. But a Russian soldier remembered he'd sold him coffee and set him free.

In 1946, Egon came to London, first as a restaurant manager, then to open restaurants. Through the auspices of an admirer, the wonderfully named Fanny Cradock, cook and food critic of the day, Egon, too, became a food critic. Now that he's gone, there are no critics left that mean anything. He led the way to improve British culinary standards with his restaurant The Marquee in Knightsbridge. He served classical French dishes that were almost unknown in Great Britain. But he served simple food. Not the elaborate plate decoration that passes for cooking excellence nowadays.

In 1955, he sold his restaurant to concentrate on his writing and then his food guides. After he became a critic, Egon said, "There is an annoying new trend for complicated menus that are anything but customer friendly. They read like recipes, with the result that you choose halibut and then fail to find it on your plate. It's even hard to get a decent dessert, instead you get a sculpture. It's ridiculous. Kitchen hands are turned into sculptors, painters, decorators, the essential subject being unrecognisably disguised. Food has no nationality, food is either good or it isn't. Anyone thunderstruck by newness alone is the worst kind of ignorant food snob."

Egon was not a snob – although he was of course horrified by the communal teaspoon he once found attached to a string hanging above the sugar bowl at a café in a London railway station. When, 15 years ago, I started writing tales about my life in restaurants – some people aggrandise these vignettes by saying I'm a food critic – I was greeted with contempt and hostility by other food writers. Not so Egon. He rang to congratulate me and we often spoke and met thereafter. He was a marvellous supporter. It made me very proud.

His views on the unnecessary complications of food, menus and restaurant staff presentation coincided exactly with my own. Egon had been determined, through example, and through his Egon Ronay

Guides, to improve catering standards in England. He said, "I think my guides have had the effect of telling people in mass catering that they could no longer get away with murder – because I would expose them."

There's no question Egon improved standards at all levels of catering in Great Britain. He couldn't go so far as to transform the profit in mass-produced food which comes from central depots and flies out of them like garbage on to plates in restaurants all over the country.

What he did was educate people as to what good could be – and thus the British, slow to rise from anonymity, started to complain more often and more vociferously about what they were eating. This was a considerable advance on diners accepting anything they were offered. But Egon would come to despair over the cult of the so-called celebrity chef. He said, "Gordon Ramsay and Jamie Oliver are not chefs any more, they are business people. They're not as good as they used to be. They don't cook. They're interested in and concerned with money. Celebrity chefs are purely a show. The word celebrity doesn't say much about merit." How right he was.

Egon was an immaculately dressed, sparkling man with wonderful wit and observation, devoid of pomp and arrogance. His Ronay Guides to restaurants and hotels were the best, far more reliable than the snooty Michelin Guides. They have never been surpassed. Strangely, when they went out of business in the 1980's, I was approached and offered hundreds of thousands of pounds to put my name on a new version of the Ronay Guide. I turned it down because (a) I could never match up to Egon and (b) I can think of little that would be more horrific than people coming up to me in the street and haranguing me because they went to a restaurant, recommended in my guide, that they didn't like.

Egon had 30 inspectors, but stayed on top of everything. He would travel round the country eating four meals a day. He'd revisit every restaurant each year, always booking under an assumed name. Like me, Egon never accepted a free meal. He had a sparkle and a great sense of humour. He unquestionably raised the standards of cooking in Great Britain.

Nowadays, people think smoking in a restaurant spoils the enjoyment of others. As a 20-cigar-a-day man, who stopped, I now agree. But Egon and I clashed in friendly fashion on TV when he defended smoking in restaurants and I, poacher turned gamekeeper, was against it.

As with every time I met Egon, it was simply wonderful to hear his news and views, often bordering on severely scandalous, about various chefs. Some he liked. Some he'd gone off. A few he still admired. The world has moved on a long way from the meat and two veg which sat on your plate in the 1940's and 1950's. Strange though it may seem, I look back with nostalgia to Second World War food – it was immensely plain, but at least the ingredients were not over chemicalised and deep frozen to a tasteless death, as so much is today.

The 1950's showed things getting a bit more daring. Then along came Egon and he led the way to continental cooking styles that started to change everything. By the 1960's, food had become adventurous. Food of different nationalities featured more and more. We'd graduated to the more carefully prepared and adventurous food that Egon both served and later encouraged in others.

This led to ever-increasing standards in the 1970's, 1980's and 1990's, but this advance was not without drawbacks. Restaurants saved on space as prices and rents rose. People were jammed closer and closer together, noise levels became horrific and the food quality in many cases took a dive. Profit before pride.

Egon looked with considerable despair at the over-complicated pomposity of menus and dishes served today. He believed that chefs should reconnect with tradition, not go into outer space in a pilotless rocket.

There are people who you may not see every day, who you may not speak to more than a dozen times a year, but whose presence in your life, even if not central, is of immense value. Thus Egon Ronay figured in my life. His notes of congratulation if he liked something I'd written, his phone calls, his gossip, I will miss them all. But, above all, the so-called hospitality industry (misnamed if any industry ever was) has lost a beacon, a guiding light. Egon Ronay was a force for good, civility, humour – and for excellence in the provision of food. Because of Egon Ronay, we all eat better than we would have done had he never fled from Russian domination of Hungary.

I miss you, Egon. I'll try to carry the Ronay flag onwards and upwards.

(reprinted from *The Daily Mail* by kind permission of Michael Winner)